D0933815

PRAISE FOR
THE FOREX TRADING MANUAL

The Forex Trading Manual is a concise, detailed, no-nonsense resource for new entrants into the Foreign Exchange market. Highly recommended.

—JAMIE COLEMAN, Managing Editor, ForexLive.com

Javier Paz coaches readers on how to trade consistently with a disciplined approach and how to recondition your trading habits if you're an experienced retail trader in search of better results. The chapters that tackle trading psychology truly set this book apart.

—DEAN POPPLEWELL, Chief Currency Analyst at OANDA

I think *The Forex Trading Manual* has hit the ball out of the park—a real home-run. We have long needed explicit instructions on the trading plan all the gurus say we need, and here it is.

—BARBARA ROCKEFELLER, author of
Technical Analysis for Dummies

This book is excellent. It brings trading to the general public, explaining it with simple words. Once the theory is over, Javier takes up on the practical side of trading, a matter often dismissed in most books. In it, I have found inspiration for my own tries.

—ARNAUD JEULIN, Founder of forexticket.com

Javier Paz's *The Forex Trading Manual* is packed with solid and sensible guidance on tackling the vast forex market. The book focuses on one of the most important aspects of successful trading—creating and following a strict trading plan.

—JAMES CHEN, CTA, CMT, Director of
Technical Research and Education at FXDD

The Forex Trading Manual will get new traders where they need to go by stripping out the fluff and just concentrating on the strategies and trading behaviors that can make a difference.

—**JOHN JAGERSON**, author of *All About Investing in Gold*

Javier has created something fairly unique with *The Forex Trading Manual*. Along with providing an introduction to forex, he offers a very specific and detailed approach to trading, including a fully outlined trading system.

—**JOHN FORMAN**, Senior Forex Analyst—Thomson Reuters, author of *The Essentials of Trading*

Javier has written a guide for Forex that is like no other; it contains all the knowledge a currency trader should possess. I would recommend this book to anyone who does not have mastery of the currency markets.

—**CASEY STUBBS**, founder of WinnersEdgeTrading.com

The Forex Trading Manual

The Rules-Based Approach to Making Money Trading Currencies

Javier H. Paz

New York   Chicago   San Francisco   Lisbon   London   Madrid   Mexico City
Milan   New Delhi   San Juan   Seoul   Singapore   Sydney   Toronto

The *McGraw·Hill* Companies

1 2 3 4 5 6 7 8 9 0   QFR/QFR   1 8 7 6 5 4 3 2

ISBN: 978-0-07-178292-0
MHID: 0-07-178292-3

e-book ISBN: 978-0-07-178293-7
e-book MHID: 0-07-178293-1

Interior design by THINK Book Works

This publication is designed to provide accurate and authoritative information in regard to the subject matter covered. It is sold with the understanding that neither the author nor the publisher is engaged in rendering legal, accounting, or other professional service. If legal advice or other expert assistance is required, the services of a competent professional person should be sought.
> —*From a Declaration of Principles Jointly Adopted by a Committee of the American Bar Association and a Committee of Publishers and Associations*

The S&P 500® index ("Index") is a product of S&P Dow Jones Indices LLC and/or its affiliates. All rights reserved. For more information on any of S&P Dow Jones Indices LLC's indices please visit www.spdji.com. S&P® and S&P 500® are registered trademarks of Standard & Poor's Financial Services LLC and Dow Jones® is a registered trademark of Dow Jones Trademark Holdings LLC. S&P Dow Jones Indices LLC. Standard & Poor's Financial Services LLC, Dow Jones Trademark Holdings LLC and their respective affiliates ("S&P Dow Jones Indices") makes no representation or warranty, express or implied, as to the ability of any index to accurately represent the market, generally, or any asset class or market sector that it purports to represent and S&P Dow Jones Indices shall have no liability for any errors or omissions of any index or the data included therein. Past performance of an index is not an indication of future results. All information provided by S&P Dow Jones Indices is general in nature and not tailored to the needs of any person, entity or group of persons. S&P Dow Jones Indices LLC is not an investment advisor. S&P Dow Jones Indices does not sponsor, endorse, sell, promote or manage any investment fund or other investment vehicle or product that seeks to provide an investment return based on the performance of any index, including the S&P 500® index.

McGraw-Hill books are available at special quantity discounts to use as premiums and sales promotions, or for use in corporate training programs. To contact a representative please e-mail us at bulksales@mcgraw-hill.com.

This book is printed on acid-free paper.

Eli
Thinking of you

ACKNOWLEDGMENTS

There are special people around us. I'm referring to those who inspire us, coach us, and stand by our sides as we move forward and to new destinations. From time to time, they need to hear how much they mean to us.

I reserve a special thanks to my dear wife and to *mes enfants sauvages*, to my parents and grandparents for their patience and for being that kind of people to me.

Very special thanks to John Bas (a great man whose soul now rests in peace), Hal Heaton, and Harry Moumdjian for your selfless support. Randy Clyde, Rob Nydegger, and Roger Clarke, you have my appreciation for being mentors and people I could look up to early in my career.

I wish to thank two great friends, Jared Limon and Cason Cusack, for their help in nurturing a love for statistics and this book project. I have thoroughly enjoyed being acquainted with talented and reputable individuals in the Forex world, many of whom have contributed encouraging remarks and shared their insights: Barbara Rockefeller, John Jagerson, James Chen, Arnaud Jeulin, John Forman, Andrei Knight, Jamie Coleman, Dean Popplewell, Casey Stubbs,

Emmanuelle Girodet, Rodolfo Festa Bianchet, Dave Lemont, Yoni Assia, Matthias Beckmann, Stephen Bernard, Charles Jago, Marilyn McDonald, Ken Trionfo, and Tom O'Reilly.

Finally, a very special thanks goes to Aite Group, including Alois Pirker, Sang Lee, Frank Rizza, Jerry Clemente, Gwenn Bezard, and my many wonderful colleagues and friends.

Forex trading is risky.

The risk is high because the revenue potential is also high. Foreign exchange markets* are huge and exiting. Aite Group and the Bank for International Settlements (BIS) estimate that more than US$4.5 trillion changes hands each day in currency markets. But it would be a big mistake to think that just because this market is large, new traders will have an easy time learning to make money. The *Forex Trading Manual* is a book based on the notion that if you are to become a proficient forex trader, planning is required.

Most of the rules and perspectives of trading you will learn will be applicable to anything you trade in the future: forex, stocks, options, futures, or commodities. This book happens to be about forex because I have a special fondness for currency markets, which have unique attributes that are not seen in other markets.

I have written plenty of institutional forex briefings and industry reports, but this book is written in a familiar tone

* Also known as forex, FX, and foreign currency

and language. I hope that this approach will make the topic interesting to younger audiences and nonfinancial experts, as well as to those individuals who are already familiar with trading.

Anyone who has traveled to a foreign country understands the need to exchange currencies at the airport or at a bank. My first *real* encounter with currency markets was early in my professional career, when I was doing export sales. As a freshly minted college grad, I worked for a small U.S. manufacturer of conference equipment. The company was trying to establish itself in foreign markets, and I was put in charge of sales to Brazilian five-star hotels. I had an ambitious sales goal that I didn't quite reach for reasons that were beyond my control. I lost export sales when Brazil's currency (the Brazilian real) declined in value and made my bids too expensive for local buyers.

That's when I began asking myself what makes currencies change in value relative to one another. If only they would stay steady or change in my favor, I thought.

After attending business school, I went on to work for a Wall Street bank, researching the behavior of foreign currencies. In that role, I advised institutional investors and corporations how to stay ahead of currency risks. A few years later, I became the institutional sales director of IBFX, a U.S. retail FX broker. In this position, I learned many valuable lessons by monitoring the trading activity of individuals who traded the money either of a fund or of several individuals.

These *money managers*, as they are called, won and lost small fortunes trading currency markets. One of them, for example, was a fellow from Chile who had a remarkable track record of no losing trades for six months. The capital he had under management grew rapidly from a few thousand dollars to about $3 million. His earnings for managing these accounts to profitability were a healthy $30,000 to $40,000 per month. I could tell that he had a genuine ability to generate trading profits consistently, but I also started to recognize his Achilles' heel. He was so focused on having a zero-loss track record that he left open a few negative trades for days. He hoped to close them at a profit when currency prices turned around—and prices often do turn around. However, he was eventually forced to close them, and these large losses crippled his master account. He was done being a money manager.

I could give many examples of fortunes won and lost. Ultimately, this book is an effort to convey what I have learned from my mistakes as a trader and others' mistakes so that the reader, if he or she is wise, will not repeat them.

This book is intended for individuals of different ages and from all walks of life who are open to learning new ways of wealth creation. The earlier in life a person learns to trade properly, the better. I would go so far as to state that the best time to start trading is while a person is in her late-teenage years, under the guidance of a responsible adult.

Trading currencies has the appeal of a game that you can get to be really good at without ever feeling like it has become too predictable. I love the intellectual challenge, the fun of self-mastery, and the healthy return on investment that is achievable.

After you read this book, you will be at a great advantage relative to individuals who have a piecemeal approach to learning to trade. These people hear about online trading, get excited, get some bits of useful trading information here and there, and start to trade with a live account before too long. And invariably they start losing more than they manage to earn. If they are persistent, these dear losses will teach them a healthy respect for learning to trade "the right way."

This is a book about learning to trade the right way, by

- Understanding the basics of trading
- Looking at the big picture of what it takes to succeed
- Following a reliable trading plan to reach the summit

My definition of a trader's summit is relatively simple but not easy to achieve. It is learning to have more wins than losses, keeping trading losses small, and making profitable trades as large as possible.

Throughout this book, I will use a driving analogy. I believe that the effort required to learn to drive a car is similar in many ways to what a new trader has to learn in order to become proficient. Of course, there is more to trading than there is to learning to drive a car.

The trading plan is one of the strengths of this book, but I introduce it only in Chapter 8, after you feel comfortable with basic trading concepts. I want you to think of the forex trading plan as the document that helps you pass the test to become a proficient forex trader.

Chapters 1 through 4 cover the mechanics of trading, including lessons on risk management. Chapter 5 gives you an introduction to technical analysis, and Chapter 6 gives you a comprehensive understanding of fundamental analysis. Chapter 7 teaches you in detail a very effective trading strategy called the Pivot Roadmap. Becoming a successful trader requires a profound change of perspective, and Chapter 9 will help you to make that transition; this is what I call mental conditioning. In Chapter 10, I identify the resources that can ease the path for a trader to become successful.

Chapter 11 offers a robust guide to various resources traders need to be efficient. Finally, Chapter 12 sums up the key takeaways of each chapter and offers some parting thoughts. If you have the inclination to do so, reading the final chapter before reading the book may give you a sense of how the book's contents are organized.

I offer plenty of examples throughout the book to tackle technical topics, but if you feel a little stuck on any particular section, carry on and come back to it later.

Similarities Between Driving and Trading

THE FOREX DRIVER ANALOGY

The fear of driving under adverse weather conditions can have a paralyzing effect on new drivers. Picture a 15-year-old boy inside a car that is parked in front of his house, grasping the steering wheel with excitement. He is months away from getting his driver's license and being able to offer a ride home to cute and excitable girls. This happens to be an insecure teen, one who is prone to thoughts of remote risks. He now imagines himself driving on the freeway on a rainy day next to a semitrailer truck that is dumping copious amounts of water on his car's windshield. There is zero visibility at 60 miles per hour. His heart rate is accelerating; his eyes are fixed ahead. His grip on that steering wheel has suddenly gotten pretty tight.

To a lot more people than you might imagine, learning forex trading can be as scary as the thought of sharing the road with a water-gushing truck was to this boy. What could we tell our imaginary 15-year-old to stop him from hyperventilating? We can start by reminding him that those scenarios are everyday occurrences, but in very few instances do they actually lead to accidents. The key to keeping one's wits about one in that situation can be as simple as (1) gradually slowing down, (2) not making sudden lane changes, and (3) turning on the hazard lights.

Driving cars is an activity that most adults have adopted. Yet, nobody would say that being behind the wheel is always easy. Driving requires concentration and coordination. We concentrate on the road, on other vehicles, and on driving conditions. Like big computers, drivers are expected to calculate in real time the distance to the car in front of them, keep open the possibility that another driver might do something foolish, and so on.

As drivers, we are also required to maintain a delicate coordination among our eyes, our left hand on the wheel, our right hand on the stick, and our foot on the right pedal. Some people would argue that the reason we drive automatic cars is so that we can hold a phone to send that important text or Twitter update: "omg, I just crashed. ☹☹"

Learning to trade forex also requires concentration and coordination. You will learn to shut out life's distractions and the noise from news headlines and to focus on charts that will tell you whether or not to place a trade. You will also learn how to set the proper trade size, take-profit levels, and stop-loss levels.

Lack of patience is one of the biggest enemies that we will work on defeating. In fact, some of you are probably already wondering when I will get to "the good stuff." By design, I am starting this book with some mental conditioning before we jump to the technical chapters. For those of you who have watched *The Karate Kid*, this is a *wax on, wax off,* moment.

FOREX DRIVING SCHOOL

This book will teach you how to become a proficient forex driver in what I believe is the proper sequence. Each chapter prepares you for the next lesson, so I strongly recommend that you read the book in order.

It's been a while since I was in driving school. One of the few things I remember about the experience was sitting in a driving simulator while my driving instructor, a guy in his fifties with a receding hairline who spoke with a soft, monotone voice, went through the lesson. In retrospect, I think each of the students in my class had faith that we could get through driving school relatively easily. After all, if those in the previous generation had gotten their driver's licenses this way, so could each of us. Likewise, I need you to keep this type of open mind on the idea that this book can be your driving school for trading forex.

Like driving school, learning forex will require reading and practicing over the course of several months. But even though it will take some time for you to master the material, I hope the knowledge you get will make it a fun, predictable, and profitable experience.

By the end of this book, you will be surprised at how much you have learned, and you will feel empowered to go out and try forex trading on a practice account. I encourage you to trade daily, for 20 to 30 minutes each time (or more, if possible).

BASIC COMPETENCY AND EXPERT HANDLING

There is something to be said about managing our own expectations of what we can achieve as forex traders, both initially and over time. Many forex traders have quite high return expectations (see Figure 1-1).

FIGURE 1-1 **Monthly Return Expected by Forex Traders, 2010**

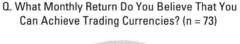

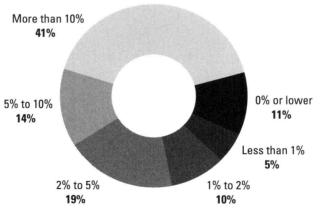

Source: Forex Datasource, 2010 online survey of 1,050 respondents from around the world, of which 73 were asked this question.

Two of every five respondents in a 2010 Forex Datasource survey expected to earn a monthly profit of more than 10 percent. This figure is surprisingly high, considering that most traditional investments today have a hard time offering a 10 percent return per *year*. The 10 percent per month figure should also be taken with caution. With higher-than-average return comes higher-than-average risk of loss. Achieving that type of return is possible, but it is not as easy or quick as many traders initially expect. In Figure 1-2, a separate survey of global traders commissioned by CitiFX Pro (a Citibank unit) shows whether these high expectations of forex traders were achieved. About 27 percent of respondents lost money for the year, and a select 11 percent of traders reported an annual return of more than 100 percent; the majority of traders were somewhere in between.

FIGURE 1-2 Past Performance of Forex Traders, 2010

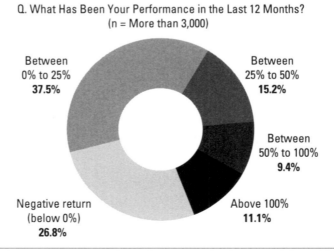

Q. What Has Been Your Performance in the Last 12 Months?
(n = More than 3,000)

Between 0% to 25%
37.5%

Between 25% to 50%
15.2%

Between 50% to 100%
9.4%

Negative return (below 0%)
26.8%

Above 100%
11.1%

Source: CitiFX Pro, 2010 survey of more than 3,000 traders from around the world.

So what should be your expected trading performance? This is a trick question. Setting a return target is secondary to becoming a proficient, disciplined trader.

When the State of Utah granted me a driver's license at age 16, it didn't expect me to be ready to race cars in Formula 1 events or to do crazy turns and jumps the way a Hollywood stunt driver would. My license was the last step in a process where I had shown a *basic understanding of and proficiency at* driving a car under normal conditions.

When the state grants driver's licenses, it has no certainty that all new drivers will be proficient drivers. Our society, from state agencies to insurance companies, has developed a fairly sophisticated system for educating, authorizing, and insuring drivers. It has also devised methods for removing, temporarily or permanently, drivers who are considered to be dangerous. Thus, it could be said that our society takes calculated risks on the driving population.

The goal of this book is to help you take calculated trading risks and become a proficient trader. With additional time, education, and dedication, a proficient trader becomes an *expert* trader.

THE RANKS OF FOREX TRADERS ARE GROWING

Aite Group estimates that the number of people who are interested in forex trading (those with live and practice trading accounts) grew to more than 28 million worldwide, with much of the growth taking place in Europe and Asia (see Figure 1-3).

FIGURE 1-3 **Geographic Location of FX Online Visitors to Broker Websites, 2011**

Geographic Location of FX Online Visitors to Broker Websites
(In thousands of unique visitors; n = 28.2 million)

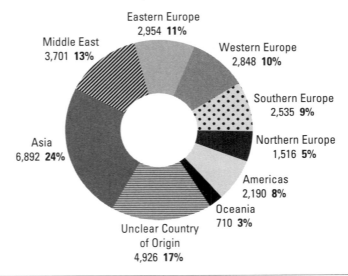

Eastern Europe
2,954 **11%**

Middle East
3,701 **13%**

Western Europe
2,848 **10%**

Southern Europe
2,535 **9%**

Asia
6,892 **24%**

Northern Europe
1,516 **5%**

Americas
2,190 **8%**

Oceania
710 **3%**

Unclear Country
of Origin
4,926 **17%**

Source: Aite Group.

People in Japan have taken on forex trading the most strongly. The Financial Futures Association of Japan reports that, as of March 2012, there are more than 3.9 million forex trading accounts in Japan. In an October 2009 article, the respected business journal *Financial Times* reported that Japanese forex traders included "everyone from housewives to full time workers who have given up their day jobs to focus on currency trading."[1]

Growth of retail forex in the United States has been considerable, but it has been somewhat slower than in other parts of the world. There are clear signs that FX trading is growing in the United States as well, however. Each year, *Inc.* magazine recognizes the fastest-growing privately held firms in the United States. These companies typically show three-year revenue growth rates in excess of 100 percent. Every year from 2004 through 2011, *Inc.* recognized at least one U.S. forex trading firm in its prestigious list: FXCM (2004, 2005, 2006, 2010), Global Futures & Forex (2006, 2007, 2008), FX Solutions (2007, 2008), Gain Capital (2007, 2008, 2009), CMS Forex (2007, 2008, 2009), Interbank FX (2008, 2009), Forex Club (2010), and Boston Technologies (2011).

It is also interesting to observe that if the forex trading business depended on a good economy to thrive, we would not have seen these firms post record revenue growth during the 2007 to 2011 period.

Virtually all of this forex trading growth has taken place since 2005, although its roots date back to the late 1990s. What do traders find attractive in forex trading? One-third of the traders surveyed by CitiFX Pro believed that forex trading offers the best potential return in both up and down markets (see Figure 1-4). Stock and bond markets are acting in unpredictable ways associated with changing economic and political conditions.

The forex market has thrived regardless of whether the global economy was booming or was in the midst of a severe crisis. Forex trading is also attractive because people who trade it find it interesting and convenient to trade—it is open 24 hours per day for 5.5 days a week.

FIGURE 1-4 Main Reasons for Trading Forex, 2010

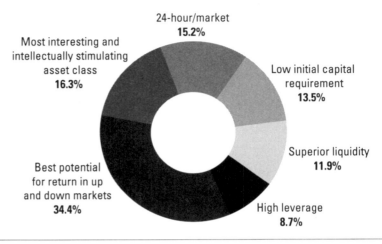

Q. What is The Strongest Reason For You To Trade FX?
(n = more than 3,000)

24-hour/market
15.2%

Most interesting and
intellectually stimulating
asset class
16.3%

Low initial capital
requirement
13.5%

Superior liquidity
11.9%

Best potential
for return in up
and down markets
34.4%

High leverage
8.7%

Source: CitiFX Pro.

Important Terminology in Forex Trading

Let's move closer to trading and start to get technical. If you are already a trader, I recommend that you skim over my definitions of terms (like leverage, margin utilization, and so on) and make sure that your foundation of these trading terms is rock solid. If you are completely new to trading, then pay close attention.

The experience of driving a car is measured using some technical terms that may not be understood by those who do not drive. For example, if we asked a 12-year-old kid to define the meaning and use of mph, rpm, or psi, the kid would probably struggle a bit.

We measure travel speed and distance in miles per hour (mph). When we press the gas pedal, we measure rotational speed within the engine in terms of revolutions per minute (rpm). And we measure tire pressure in terms of pounds per square inch (psi). There are recommended numeric ranges for each of these measures.

In this chapter, we explain a few key concepts that will allow a new forex trader to appreciate what forex trading is all about. Very importantly, this is where we will cover how we measure trading profit and loss.

WHAT IS FOREX?

Forex is the name given to a very large market that involves buying one currency and selling another currency simultaneously. An exchange of currencies occurs anytime a person or entity in one country goes through the process of acquiring the currency of another country to

- Buy goods or services from a foreign company
- Hedge (protect) a foreign investment or trade receivable
- Buy foreign securities
- Borrow money from foreign investors
- Pay for meals and transportation while on a vacation abroad
- Speculate on changing foreign currency rates

Since the end of the Cold War era (approximately 1991), international trade and investment have increased at an extremely rapid pace. Money flowing within international money and capital markets is now measured in the hundreds of trillions of U.S. dollars. The daily trading volume of the forex market, as measured by the Bank for International

Settlements and Aite Group, has risen from US$1.2 trillion per day in 2001 to approximately US$4.5 trillion in 2011.

Currency trading can be dated back thousands of years ago, originating in a need to exchange diverse commodities like grain, spices, and wine outside of a local or national region.[1] However, it was only in the late 1990s that, through advances in trading technology and the Internet, individuals gained the ability to participate in this very large and fast-growing market. Although $4.5 trillion trades daily in forex markets, Aite Group estimates that more than US$350 billion per day changes hands in the retail part of the FX market.

CURRENCY PAIRS

In many markets, there are thousands of securities that someone could trade. Not so in forex markets, where the task of deciding what to trade is much simpler. Currency trading occurs in pairs, that is, currency pairs. There are seven currency pairs that people trade the most: EURUSD, GBPUSD, USDJPY, USDCHF, USDCAD, AUDUSD, and NZDUSD.

For example, EURUSD represents the value of one euro measured in U.S. dollars. If the current price of EURUSD is 1.3203, this means that for every euro, we get one dollar, 32 cents (or pennies), and three hundredths of a penny. When you go to a bank to exchange dollars for euros, you never get these hundredths of a penny (called pips), but when you trade forex, these pips matter a great deal.

Just to solidify the concept of currency pairs, let's do one more example. The USDJPY pair represents the value of one U.S. dollar measured in Japanese yen. If the current price of USDJPY is 89.95, this means that for every U.S. dollar, we should get 89 yen and 95 cents.

In these two examples, the U.S. dollar appears in different positions within the pair. The first three letters of a currency pair represent the *base currency*, while the latter three letters represent the *quote currency*. It is a good idea to memorize the order of the currency pairs, because they follow conventions or common usages.

You would not say that your vehicle was traveling at 45 miles per "half an hour." Similarly, most forex traders would not quote the value of the U.S. dollar measured in euros, or USDEUR. It just isn't proper. Likewise, we would never quote yen measured in U.S. dollars, or JPYUSD. The most practical approach is to commit to memory the currency pairs in Table 2-1. The seven most common currency pairs are those that trade against the U.S. dollar—in other words, they all have "USD" in the currency pair.

There are also FX trading instruments called "cross-currency" pairs in which the U.S. dollar is not one of the two currencies in the pair. The most common of these "crosses" appear in Table 2-2.

Most of the Forex trading volume occurs in a few currency pairs, as shown in Table 2-3. Approximately 73 percent of all trading is done in the nine currency pairs listed in Table 2-3.

TABLE 2-1 Major Currency Pairs

CURRENCY PAIR	VALUE	NICKNAME	COUNTRIES
EURUSD	Number of U.S. dollars for one euro	Euro-dollar, fiber	Eurozone region/ United States
GBPUSD	Number of U.S. dollars for one British pound sterling	Pound-dollar, sterling-dollar, cable	Great Britain/ United States
USDJPY	Number of Japanese yen for one U.S. dollar	Dollar-yen, ninja	United States/ Japan
USDCHF	Number of Swiss francs for one U.S. dollar	Dollar-franc, swissie	United States/ Switzerland
USDCAD	Number of Canadian dollars for one U.S. dollar	Dollar-Canadian, loonie, the funds	United States/ Canada
AUDUSD	Number of U.S. dollars for one Australian dollar	Aussie-dollar, Matie	Australia/United States
NZDUSD	Number of U.S. dollars for one New Zealand dollar	Kiwi-dollar	New Zealand/ United States

TABLE 2-2 Other Currency Pairs—Crosses and Selected Pairs

CURRENCY PAIR	VALUE	NICKNAME	COUNTRIES
EURJPY	Number of Japanese yen for one euro	Euro-yen, Euppy, Yuppi	Eurozone region/ Japan
EURGBP	Number of British pounds sterling for one euro	Euro-pound, Euro sterling, Chunnel	Eurozone region/ Great Britain
EURCHF	Number of Swiss francs for one euro	Euro-Swissie	Eurozone region/ Switzerland
GBPCHF	Number of Swiss francs for one British pound sterling	Pound-Swissie, Cable-Swissie	Great Britain/ Switzerland
GBPJPY	Number of Japanese yen for one British pound sterling	Pound-Yen, Geppie	Great Britain/Japan
AUDJPY	Number of Japanese yen for one Australian dollar	Aussie-Yen	Australia/Japan
AUDNZD	Number of New Zealand dollars for one Australian dollar	Aussie-Kiwi	Australia/New Zealand
EURAUD	Number of euros for one Australian dollar	Euro-Aussie	Eurozone region/ Australia
AUDCAD	Number of Canadian dollars for one Australian dollar	Aussie-Loonie	Australia/Canada

TABLE 2-3 Currency Pairs by Daily Volume, 2001 to 2010

CURRENCY PAIR	2001 US$BN	2001 SHARE	2004 US$BN	2004 SHARE	2007 US$BN	2007 SHARE	2010 US$BN	2010 SHARE
EURUSD	$372	30%	$541	28%	$892	27%	$1,101	28%
USDJPY	$250	20%	$328	17%	$438	13%	$568	14%
GBPUSD	$129	10%	$259	13%	$384	12%	$360	9%
AUDUSD	$51	4%	$107	6%	$185	6%	$249	6%
USDCHF	$59	5%	$83	4%	$151	5%	$168	4%
USDCAD	$54	5%	$77	4%	$126	4%	$182	5%
EURJPY	$36	3%	$61	3%	$86	3%	$111	3%
EURGBP	$27	2%	$47	2%	$69	2%	$109	3%
EURCHF	$13	1%	$30	2%	$62	2%	$72	2%
USD—Other	$200	16%	$308	15%	$669	21%	$750	19%
EUR—Other	$22	1%	$44	2%	$123	3%	$163	4%
Other currency pairs	$28	2%	$50	3%	$139	4%	$149	4%
All currency pairs	$1,239		$1,934		$3,324		$3,981	

PIPS: THE BASIS OF FOREX TRADING MEASUREMENTS

In the previous section, I mentioned that a pip (which stands for *percentage in point*) is one of the smallest measures of change in currency prices.

For example, when the price of EURUSD (the euro-dollar pair) moves from 1.3345 to 1.3346, we are talking about a 1-pip movement. Similarly, when the price of USDJPY (the dollar-yen pair) moves from 89.21 to 89.22, we are also talking about a 1-pip movement.

So what is the relevance of pips? Most forex traders measure their trading gains and losses in pips. The value of pips may vary depending on the (1) currency pair, (2) current price of the pair, and (3) type of trading account: standard account or mini account.

Many people start trading forex using so-called mini accounts, with a starting deposit of $250 to $2,500. For mini accounts, the pip value averages a little more than $1.00. Standard accounts have minimum deposits of $2,500 or higher, and the average pip value is a little more than $10.00. But it is important to note that not all currency pairs have the same pip value—see Table 2-4.

Table 2-4 shows the pip value (in U.S. dollars) for many currency pairs and crosses, based on December 30, 2011, prices. In practical terms, you want to become familiar with the pip value for the specific currency pairs that you would like to trade. Most people trade the euro against the dollar. Something interesting to note is that the EURUSD pip

TABLE 2-4 Sample Pip Values, 2011

CURRENCY PAIR	PIP VALUE		CURRENCY PAIR	PIP VALUE	
	STANDARD ACCOUNT	MINI ACCOUNT		STANDARD ACCOUNT	MINI ACCOUNT
EURUSD	$10.00	$1.00	NZDUSD	$10.00	$1.00
USDJPY	$12.99	$1.30	AUDNZD	$7.78	$0.78
GBPUSD	$10.00	$1.00	EURAUD	$10.22	$1.02
AUDUSD	$10.00	$1.00	AUDJPY	$12.99	$1.13
USDCHF	$10.64	$1.06	CHFJPY	$12.99	$1.13
EURJPY	$12.99	$1.13	NZDJPY	$12.99	$1.13
GBPJPY	$12.99	$1.13	AUDCAD	$9.82	$0.98
EURCHF	$10.64	$1.06	AUDCHF	$10.64	$1.06
EURGBP	$15.53	$1.55	GBPCAD	$9.82	$0.98
EURCAD	$9.82	$0.98	EURNZD	$7.78	$0.78
USDCAD	$9.82	$0.98	GBPCHF	$10.64	$1.06

value is *always* $10 ($1 if you have a mini account). There are three other major currencies that have a never-changing pip value of $10 against the dollar: GBPUSD, AUDUSD, and NZDUSD.

The pip value for the yen, the Swiss franc, and the Canadian dollar will change over time, as will the pip value of currency crosses. To find the precise currency pip value at any given time, there are pip-value calculators on the Internet that you can use.

Please note that most pip values range between $9 and $12, but there is one pair, EURGBP, that has a pip value of $15.53 and possibly higher. What this means is that you need to be careful when you are setting your profit target and stop-loss levels in euro sterling. For a regular pair, setting a

20- or 30-pip profit target or stop-loss level will be around $200 to $300, but in EURGBP, a 20- to 30-pip target/stop-loss level represents $350 to $450.

MAKING MONEY BUYING OR SELLING

This section covers the simple mechanics of buying and selling currency contracts, which includes how money is made or lost trading currencies.

For a proficient forex trader, a basic task is to determine the currency price direction over a certain period: will the price of a currency pair go up or down? You also need to determine how much the currency price might go up or down, and possibly how long it might take to get to the target price.

For example, if you believe that the price of EURUSD will rise (the euro will go up and the dollar down), you would *buy* EURUSD and wait to see if the market confirms your expectation. So, let's say you buy one standard contract (also called one *standard lot*) of euro dollar at, say, 1.3240. Let's further say that the price on this contract rises to 1.3255, at which point you decide to close the trade. The resulting profit is +15 pips (1.3255 − 1.3240 = 0.0015). The dollar value for that 15-pip gain would be $150 (15 pips × $10 standard lot pip value × 1 standard lot). If you are trading 2 standard lots, then the same 15-pip gain represents a $300 gain (15 × $10 × 2).

Now let's consider what happens if you are wrong about the direction of the euro dollar. Let's say you buy three *mini* lots of EURUSD at 1.3240, and you decide to allow a maximum loss of 20 pips for the trade. This time, the dollar strengthens, and EURUSD drops 20 pips, triggering a loss for the trade. How much did you lose on this trade? The calculation would be

−20 pips × $1 mini lot pip value × 3 mini lots = −$60

In a different example, let's say that you believe the price of euro dollar will fall over the foreseeable future, so you *sell* EURUSD (sell euros and buy U.S. dollars). But wait a minute. You don't *own* euros in real life, so you ask yourself how it is that you can sell them if you don't already own them. Well, when trading forex, it is possible to make money if the price of a currency pair goes up or down, whether you own it in real life or not. When you trade forex, you are trading *contracts*, not crisp bills of domestic or foreign currency.

So, back to the second example, you believe that EURUSD will go down in value. Your broker allows you to enter into a two-mini-lot *sell* EURUSD contract at the order entry price, 1.3250, for example. Let's say that you are right, and the price does decrease 25 pips. You want to close the trade at that point. Essentially, it is as if you entered into a contract to sell a house before prices on the property tumbled. Because you have a contract that guarantees you a sell price of 1.3250 and the going rate is now 1.3225, you deliver the sell contract and become entitled to the difference of 25 pips. Your trading gain would be $50:

25 pips × $1 mini lot pip value × 2 mini lots = $50

In the coming chapters, you will learn some of the optimal conditions for buying and selling. Novice and intermediate traders will also learn how to overcome negative impulses that may prevent them from achieving consistent positive returns.

THE CURRENCY SPREAD AND LIQUIDITY

At any given time, a trading platform should show two prices for a currency pair, one price (the *bid*) for buyers and one price (the *ask*) for sellers. The difference between the bid and ask prices is called the *spread*. Most major currency pairs show a spread that is 2 to 3 pips wide. Why is there a need for bid *and* ask prices when we could have one price? The bid and ask prices remind us that there is a cost for the convenience of having someone (a bank or broker) say *"buy"* whenever a trader says *"sell."*

What is liquidity? We can define *liquidity* as the availability of buyers and sellers at any given point. On eBay, when many people are bidding for an item, the bidding price increases in small increments. Together, these buyers are discovering the true price of an item and are providing liquidity in the process. If an eBay auction has few participants, the price is all over the place. Liquidity is spotty and low.

In currency markets, brokers set a wide spread on currencies that are not very popular and a very tight spread on currencies that are. For example, a broker may set a wide spread of 10 pips on GBPNZD (sterling kiwi), but a tight (1.5-pip) spread for EURUSD.

A key point to make is that forex brokers stay in business by charging the spread. Bringing trading technology to tens of thousands of people around the world and around the clock is expensive and requires operational sophistication. Fortunately, currency spreads have decreased over time. Back in the late 1990s, the spread on EURUSD was more than 5 pips, whereas now it is between 1 and 2 pips in most cases as a result of competition among brokers. For the purposes of our discussion here, the bid price will always be lower than the ask price.

> *Sell at the bid.* The bid price is the current price at which you can sell a currency pair to your broker—*sell at the bid*. Thus, "bid" is what the broker is bidding to buy from you.

> *Buy at the ask.* Conversely, the ask price is the current price at which you can buy a currency pair—*buy at the ask*—or the price at which the broker will sell the currency pair (what the broker is asking).

For example, if GBPUSD shows a bid/ask of 1.4836 – 1.4840, this tells us first of all that the spread is 4 pips (1.4840 – 1.4836). When we get into a trade (regardless of whether we buy or sell), our standard account gets charged the spread, $40. If you have a mini account, the spread charge will be $4.

If we bought GBPUSD, the entry price for our trade would be 1.4840—the ask price. If the price goes up 2 pips, then our account balance now shows –$20. If the price continues to go up to 20 pips above the entry level, then the account balance would show a profit of $160 (20 pips × $10 × 1 lot minus a spread charge of $40). In many trades, I look for a *net profit* of 30 pips. This means that I have to earn 30 pips *plus* the cost of the spread—that could be 34 pips in the case of GBPUSD.

The currency markets move so quickly that it is quite possible that a person could recover the cost of the trade within a few minutes of trading.

Securing a Trader's Permit

A high percentage of people open real forex trading accounts prematurely, without having achieved consistent positive results in a practice account. These premature traders are asking for an emotional roller-coaster ride that should not be underestimated!

The moment that you put on a live trade, a flood of emotions—anxiety, excitement, fear, and greed—will overwhelm you if you are not prepared. Ironically, most people who trade live before it's time to do so are not quite aware of what they don't know. If they had only read this chapter.

FRIENDS DON'T LET FRIENDS GOOGLE AND TRADE LIVE

Google and search engines at large do a lot of good by getting us abundant information when we make queries. But there is a problem when we think that information is the same thing as education. There are right and wrong ways of becoming a forex trader. The biggest mistake that beginners make is doing a web search for information about forex trading, reading some "trading lessons," and assuming that they will become proficient traders just by reading what they find.

Think of it this way: imagine that you want to drive a vehicle and you find some great sites that tell you about how much fun it is to drive cars, how to leave burn tracks on the pavement, and how to approach curves really fast. The information that you learned is valid, but it puts you on track to become a thrill-seeking, reckless driver, not a proficient, safe driver.

> **KEY CONCEPT:** A proper education includes information, but there is more than just that. In my view, there are three key components of a sound forex trading education: knowledge, tools, and support.

The *knowledge* I am talking about is the basics of trading: technical analysis, rules-based strategies, and risk-management principles.

By *tools*, I am referring to trading platforms, technical indicators, news widgets, and other uses of technology that make trading easier.

Support stands for having access to someone who knows a lot about trading and who becomes a beginner's coach or mentor.

Take it from someone who has visited and evaluated several hundred forex websites: there is a lot of garbage about forex trading out there on the web.

Someone who is just starting to become familiar with forex is not prepared to discern which firms are for real and which ones aren't. There are a lot of misleading marketing claims for trading systems, education programs, broker services, and signal providers. By the time you finish reading this book, you will be better prepared to identify reputable firms.

GETTING A LEARNER'S PERMIT FOR TRADING FOREX

Here's a simple question. Why do many governments ask that new drivers get a learner's permit? A learner's permit is given when someone has demonstrated sufficient skills (1) in the driver education classroom and (2) in the simulator, and is now ready for some practice outside of the classroom. But the government is not yet ready to certify that the learner's permit holder is ready to receive a driver's license.

The moment the government issues you a driver's license, society at large assumes that you are a competent driver who will conform to traffic laws. The government also reserves the right to suspend or revoke your driving privileges if you do something really wrong.

Unfortunately, when you are learning to trade forex, there is no entity that will stop you and ask you if you know enough to start trading with real money. Nobody will check your competence as a trader, or the quality of the tools that you are using, or the credentials of your coach. Nor should the government have that role.

As a result, *you* are the one who's responsible for the quality of the education, tools, and support that you use. Fortunately, you are not alone. This book is my attempt to share with you the most useful lessons that I have picked up over the past 10-plus years in this industry.

BENEFITS OF A PRACTICE ACCOUNT

Trading on paper is another term for someone who opens a practice account.[1]

> **KEY CONCEPT:** Here is one of the biggest lessons I could ever teach you: learn to achieve consistent success trading on a practice account before you start to trade on a live account. And when you open a live account, start with a small account size ($1,000 to $5,000) before investing bigger sums.

Most people understand the basic concept that having a practice account is a good idea. Indeed, most people can probably see how a practice account can help you become familiar with the trading platform, order entry, currency price behaviors, and technical analysis tools. Unfortunately, not many people have a true appreciation that:

- A practice account can help you learn the first key lesson of forex trading done the right way: *patience.*
- A practice account can help you reach a point at which you are mentally and emotionally ready to trade with real money.

PATIENCE

The first item in the list, patience, is key. If you think about it, you had to exercise a lot of patience before you felt confident behind the wheel of a car on a busy street.

You had to sit through the training, pass the machine simulator tests, and then pass other tests in the driving range. Then came multiple supervised "road tests," and then a final test in which you demonstrated your driving proficiency to a government official.

> **KEY CONCEPT:** The forex practice account is your best friend. It will be patient when you make mistakes. It will help you gain a healthy respect for the complexity of the forex market.

We have to acknowledge that you may not be grateful for a practice account if you place a large bet and get lucky. Maybe then you will wish: "Oh, if I had done this in a real account, I'd be so happy now." Perhaps. But the forex market has a way of quickly humbling anyone who thinks that he knows more than he really does. Trust me on this one. You are much better off using a practice account for a long time than for a short time.

So what is an appropriate amount of time to spend while learning on a practice account? It depends on your ability to achieve success on a consistent, predictable basis. But there is one thing I will guarantee: applying the lessons on this book will shorten your learning curve by at least several months and improve the outcome compared to someone who learns as she goes.

Chapter 7 will teach you one specific trading strategy. Once you can put this strategy to use and attain a profitable performance of 2 to 5 percent per month, you could venture into opening a *small* live account to continue your apprenticeship.

Of course, there will be countless lessons that you will learn over time after you start trading live. But the goal of this book is to help you get to the point of trading competence and proficiency.

By the way, successful traders continue to use their practice accounts for testing new strategies long after they open a live trading account. I personally recommend that you have one trading account in which you follow all the rules that I will teach you. You will also need a separate practice account (demo 2) as an escape where you can try different strategies and currencies, and allow yourself to make breakthroughs and (why not?) place risky or impulsive trades.

FEELING MENTALLY AND EMOTIONALLY READY

The second benefit of a practice account is that it becomes a playing ground until you become sufficiently mature to deal with the stress of trading.

If you drive a car when you are in a very emotional state, is it fair to say that the odds that you might get into a dangerous situation increase? Let's say you are driving when you are

- Late for work, and you have been warned that being late one more time may result in your getting fired

- Very upset because of something that happened in the road or at home or at the office
- Distracted because you are going through the loss of someone dear or because you are having marital problems
- Behaving recklessly to *impress* other car passengers

We can all agree that all these situations put drivers at a high risk of getting into an accident and getting people hurt.

The reason is simple: driving a car is most predictable when we are alert and have our emotions in check. Trading is similar to driving in this regard. Trading is most predictable when we are alert and have our emotions in check.

We can understand perfectly someone's need to make money quickly trading forex. The need to make money is what pushes a lot of people into live forex trading prematurely. I have seen many poor souls who even borrowed money from credit cards to invest in forex trading with the hope of paying it back quickly, only to lose it all and be stuck with a huge credit card bill in addition to the financial mess they were in previously!

When you go into trading with that kind of baggage or self-imposed pressure, you are reducing the odds of success that you could have had if you had shown more patience when you were learning the materials.

To someone who is brand-new to forex and is pressed to make money quickly, I would say, look to forex as your way to financial freedom over the medium to long term—not over the short term. Treat your practice account like a night school where you are learning forex trading on a part-time basis. Learn it right, because it can really help you. If you rush your learning, you will probably not do it too well.

> **KEY CONCEPT:** A practice account allows us to understand the impact of trading when we are under various kinds of mental and emotional stresses: the excitement of a major win, the disappointment of trading losses, the anxiety of not fully understanding the behavior of market prices, and so on.

You learn these lessons better while you are on a practice account rather than trading on a live account!

SETTING PERFORMANCE TARGETS

Someone once asked Michael Jordan how he scored more than 30 points per basketball game, to which he replied that he just concentrated on making 8 points per quarter. This approach—keeping a focus on a reasonable goal and just being consistent—was critical to making him a very successful player.

We can learn a lot about setting a daily target from Michael's comment. If you do a web search for forex trading systems, you will probably find systems that supposedly produce thousands of pips per month.

So it might surprise you that I believe that you can become quite wealthy by simply averaging 20 pips per day.

Michael's goal: 8 points per quarter

Our goal: 20 pips per day

In order to get to a 20-pip average, you will need to aim for 20 to 40 pips on a given day. Some days, you will get only get 5 to 10 pips, and that is fine. Every bit counts as you aim for the goal of a net 100 pips per week (a weekly goal is another way of understanding the 20-pips-per-day average). As you can imagine, you will have days when you lose 20 to 30 pips. You should start with a weekly target of 50 pips and increase it over time as you attain the intermediate goal.

Ultimately, whether or not you can get to the weekly pip target will depend a lot on *trade execution*: trading when you should, refraining when you shouldn't trade, and gaining a trade entry at the appropriate levels. Upcoming chapters will deal with these points.

CAPITAL ACCUMULATION

Rather than constantly moving money into and out of your trading account, you should consider reinvesting your forex earnings for a period. Let's take a look at what a 10-pip-per-day average can do to the trading account of a disciplined trader. To keep things simple, we will assume that our results come from trading only one currency pair, EURUSD, where every pip earned on a mini account equals $1.00. To help you understand the information in Table 3-1, I am showing three months' worth of trading, earning an average of 10 pips per

TABLE 3-1   Potential Earnings at 50 Pips Weekly Average, 1% Account Risk

WEEK	MINI LOTS	NET DAILY PROFIT IN PIPS	NET DAILY PROFIT IN USD	WEEKLY PROFIT IN USD	CUMULATIVE BALANCE	RISK/ TRADE, % OF ACCOUNT 1% OF ACCOUNT	RISK/ TRADE, PIPS
0					$5,000		
1	1.67	10	$16.67	$83.33	$5,083	$50.00	30 pips
2	1.69	10	$16.94	$84.72	$5,168	$50.83	30 pips
3	1.72	10	$17.23	$86.13	$5,254	$51.68	30 pips
4	1.75	10	$17.51	$87.57	$5,342	$52.54	30 pips
5	1.78	10	$17.81	$89.03	$5,431	$53.42	30 pips
6	1.81	10	$18.10	$90.51	$5,521	$54.31	30 pips
7	1.84	10	$18.40	$92.02	$5,613	$55.21	30 pips
8	1.87	10	$18.71	$93.56	$5,707	$56.13	30 pips
9	1.90	10	$19.02	$95.11	$5,802	$57.07	30 pips
10	1.93	10	$19.34	$96.70	$5,899	$58.02	30 pips
11	1.97	10	$19.66	$98.31	$5,997	$58.99	30 pips
12	2.00	10	$19.99	$99.95	$6,097	$59.97	30 pips

day and never risking more than 1 percent per trade. We are starting the account with $5,000. We are assuming a maximum stop-loss level of 30 pips. For example, in Week 1, we are risking $50, and we set the trade size at 1.67 (1.7) mini lots. So if we lose 30 pips, it is $50 (30 × 1.67). We are assuming a profit of 50 pips per week, net of losses.

The thought that we are netting 10 pips and risking 30 pips does not mean that we are risking 30 pips to earn 10 pips. Rather, it means that we won more than we lost, but the net amount of the gain was an average of 10 pips per day. We could illustrate this concept with a scenario of six trades for the week and a 67 percent profitability ratio: two positive trades of 35 pips, two positive trades of 20 pips, and two negative trades of 30 pips.

70 + 40 − 60 = 50 pips = 10 net pips per day

As the balance on the account increases, we continue to risk only 1 percent. Since we don't pull out our gains, a bigger balance allows us to increase the size of each trade week by week without risking more than 1 percent. The bigger the account balance, the bigger the daily and weekly gains. Our 12-week scenario produced a $1,097 increase (22 percent) over the original account balance.

It goes without saying that as we are able to increase the weekly profit target and extend the reinvestment period, a modest US$5,000 can turn into a very considerable retirement nest egg or source of additional cash flow. In Table 3-2, we see the same concept of a net 50 pips weekly continuously reinvested over time, but assuming a 2 percent risk. Note the direct correlation between the risk assumed and the trade size in mini lots by comparing this table to Table 3-1.

Why are these sorts of returns possible in forex?

It is a combination of these factors:

- *High leverage.* Accounts are given the "credit" to buy large currency contracts, while posting only a small amount of collateral to hold that contract.
- *Discipline.* Even though 10 or 20 pips per day is not a lot, the key challenge to make these types of results possible is for a trader to become consistent and a creature of habit.
- *Proper education.* Knowledge plus tools plus support.

TABLE 3-2 Potential Earnings at 50 Pips Weekly Average, 2% Account Risk

| MONTH | MINI LOTS | NET DAILY PROFIT | | WEEKLY PROFIT | CUMULATIVE BALANCE | RISK/TRADE, % OF ACCOUNT | RISK/TRADE, PIPS |
		IN PIPS	IN USD	IN USD		2% OF ACCOUNT	
0	3.7				$5,000		
2	4.8	10.00	$48	$911	$7,411	$143	30 pips
4	6.2	10.00	$62	$1,184	$9,633	$186	30 pips
6	8.1	10.00	$81	$1,539	$12,523	$242	30 pips
8	10.5	10.00	$105	$2,001	$16,279	$315	30 pips
10	13.7	10.00	$137	$2,601	$21,162	$410	30 pips
12	17.8	10.00	$178	$3,381	$27,509	$532	30 pips
14	23.1	10.00	$231	$4,396	$35,760	$692	30 pips
16	30.0	10.00	$300	$5,714	$46,486	$900	30 pips
18	39.0	10.00	$390	$7,428	$60,429	$1,170	30 pips
20	50.7	10.00	$507	$9,656	$78,554	$1,520	30 pips
22	65.9	10.00	$659	$12,552	$102,115	$1,976	30 pips
24	85.7	10.00	$857	$16,317	$132,744	$2,569	30 pips

It is important to remember that the EURUSD, the most frequently traded currency pair, goes up and down an average of 110 to 120 pips within a day. Other currencies have daily volatility that goes as high as 350 pips. Thus, capturing 20 pips every day or ending up the week with 100 pips is quite achievable.

The Trading Simulator

Opening a practice account can be done by downloading trading platform software to your computer or mobile device or by accessing a web-based platform. In the forex trading market, there are dozens of different trading platforms, each with different features and different ways to conduct trading. Some are web-based; others are installed as programs.

Based on my research on the preferences of individuals in the forex industry, I can safely estimate that more than 55 percent of retail traders throughout the world use *one* particular trading platform, MetaTrader 4 (more commonly known as MT4). It is not the most advanced trading platform, but because MT4 enjoys such a wide acceptance by traders and brokers, I will use it throughout this book.

THE MT4 TRADING PLATFORM

You can download the MT4 trading platform shown in on Figure 4-1 from dozens of forex broker firms in the market

FIGURE 4-1 The MT4 Trading Platform, Default View

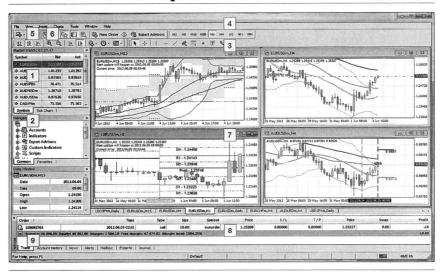

today. Each broker using the MT4 software displays its own logo and currency prices. Therefore, you may see slightly different prices in two MT4 platforms if you downloaded them from two different brokers.

> **IMPORTANT.** At the end of the book (in Appendix A), I identify the steps you can take to download an MT4 trading platform from a reputable broker. I strongly encourage you to download the MT4 platform now, before you continue studying this material, so that it will be easier to follow.

The descriptions in this section refer to the number tags seen in Figure 4-1.

Item 1. The *Market Watch* section is where the real-time, bid/ask prices of the different currency pairs are displayed. If you can't see the prices because the Market Watch box is too small, you can drag the side of the box and expand it until you can see the prices well. One of the ways to place a trade is simply by double-clicking on the currency pair of your choice in the Market Watch window, following which an order box will appear. We discuss order entry later in this chapter.

Item 2. This is the *Navigator* section. In the *Accounts* folder of the Navigator, you will be able to see multiple accounts (demo and live) that you decide to create. The *Indicators* folder contains 30 popular technical indicators that can be added to graphs simply by double-clicking on them or dragging them to a chart. The *Expert Advisors (EA)* folder is reserved for automated trading strategies that some traders like to buy, download, or create. When you activate EAs, these strategies are capable of opening and closing trades following automated rules. The *Custom Indicators* folder is similar to the Indicators folder, but it contains technical indicators that you created or purchased. The VT Pivot Roadmap Indicator, which we will talk about later, is a custom indicator.

Item 3. This section is called the *Line Studies Toolbar*. It has icons that can help you manipulate the chart in different ways, and add trend lines, Fibonacci retracements, and text to a chart.

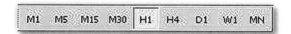

Item 4. This section, called the *Periodicity Toolbar*, displays time intervals that control the charts. M1 stands for one minute, H1 is one hour, W1 is one week, and so on. For example, when you click on these icons, you can see how a chart changes. The default periodicity in MT4 is four hours (4H). As you click on other periods, you can look for different patterns in charts of short duration (M1, M5, and M15) versus charts of longer duration.

Item 5. These three icons allow you to change to the graph type you prefer: bar graph, candlestick chart, or line graph. The candlestick chart is the default and is the most popular of the three. I discuss candlesticks a bit later in the book.

Item 6. These are the zoom buttons; they allow you to view a graph in more or less detail.

Item 7. Item 7 in Figure 4-1 is an example of a plain candlestick chart (shown here in black and white) with pivot lines. You can make a chart as simple or as complex as you desire, adding indicators and changing the colors of the candles and background. To edit the colors on the chart, right-click your mouse on top of the chart and select Properties.

NOTE. At any time, you can view and organize one or several charts. If you are displaying multiple charts, there is always one that is the "active chart." A chart becomes the one active as you click on top of it. When you make changes on items 3 to 6, the changes will reflect on the active chart. You can also maximize a single chart by clicking the maximize button on the right-hand corner, just like you would with any Windows-based object.

Order /	Time	Type	Size	Symbol	Price	S / L	T / P	Price	Swap	Profit
108093764	2012.06.05 02:31	sell	10.00	eurusdm	1.25309	0.00000	0.00000	1.25327	0.00	-18
Balance: 50 000.00 Equity: 49 982.00 Margin: 2 506.18 Free margin: 47 475.82 Margin level: 1994.35%										-18.00

Item 8. The section called *Terminal* is perhaps the most relevant of all. This is where you display important trade information (including profit and loss) and the level of risk within your account.

When a trade is open, position your mouse on top of the trade, press the right button of your mouse, and select "Profit" to display your profit or loss in either points (pips) or deposit currency (typically USD). In the picture above, I am showing the profit or loss as points, and it tells me that my trade is *down* 1.8 pips, not 18 pips.[1] These –1.8 pips times the 10 mini lots in the trade represent a "floating loss" of $18.00. Most brokers do not charge commissions, so this column will most likely be zero. The Swap column refers to the daily interest that a given trade earns or has to pay if it remains open past 5 p.m. New York time.

When you begin a trade, there will be five categories in the gray section: "Balance," "Equity," "Margin," "Free margin," and "Margin level" (when you don't have an open trade, only three categories are displayed).

- *Balance.* This is how much money there is in your account without counting profits or losses from open trades.
- *Equity.* This is how much money there would be in your account if you closed your open trades right now.
- *Margin.* This figure (also called required margin) refers to how much money or margin your broker is keeping as collateral for the trades you keep open.
- *Free margin.* This shows how much money you have that could be put to use toward a new trade.
- *Margin level.* This is one of the most important measures of risk when you have open trades. It is calculated by dividing the equity amount by the margin amount (equity/margin).

Item 9. In the Terminal section, there are other tabs that are very useful: Account History, News (available from some brokers), Alerts, Mailbox, Experts, and Journal. For example, in the Account History tab, with the right button of your mouse, you can select to save or print your trading history as Web (.html) or Excel (.csv) files.

LOT—THE BASIC CONTRACT IN CURRENCY TRADING

Now that you have the platform installed in your computer, we are almost ready to begin putting on some practice trades. First, let's get you familiar with "lots," or contract sizes.

The term *lot* is used to represent a forex contract to buy or sell a currency pair. You may say, "I bought 2 mini lots of EURUSD at 1.3104." This means that you bought two currency contracts of euros in a mini account.

Please note that you buy and sell the base currency, or, in other words, the currency that is listed *first* in a currency pair. Let's say that you think an economic announcement to be released later today will cause the U.S. dollar to lose value, and you think the Australian dollar will do well. What you could do is buy AUDUSD, which simultaneously buys Australian dollars and sells U.S. dollars.

A mini lot is a contract for 10,000 units of the base currency, while a standard lot is a contract for 100,000 units. You may be wondering, do I have to have $10,000 to $100,000 to trade forex? The answer is no, you don't.

Leverage is a feature that allows individuals with small account sizes to assume a trading contract that is much larger than the actual trading account. I will discuss leverage shortly. There are also brokers that allow traders to trade in *micro lots*, which are a tenth the size of a mini lot. Forex traders who want to move from demo to live trading sometimes use micro lots to enable them to risk a smaller portion of their account. Not all brokers allow their clients to trade in micro lots, but most allow mini and standard lots. Traders who wish to test rapid-fire automated trading systems also use micro lots extensively.

Margin Required

Let's look at the value of a standard or mini lot in the context of margin. If you have traded stocks online, then the concept of margin required will be a familiar one. But I will assume that this is the first time you have heard a formal explanation of it.

In simple terms, margin required is the part of your account that the broker will hold as collateral when you place a trade. The money in your account that is not tied up as collateral is called *free margin*. In my view, the more free margin that a trader has when there are open trades, the merrier.

Let's dive deeper by looking at an example. Say you opened a practice standard account with $5,000 at a forex brokerage firm. After you double-click on the price of the currency you wish to trade—AUDUSD in our example—a pop-up Order window appears (Figure 4-2). In the "Volume" box you enter the contract size, 1. If you opened a standard account and enter 1.00, then you are placing a trade for 1 standard lot. Conversely, if you enter 0.1, it means that you want 1 mini lot. If you opened a mini account, however, and you enter 1.0, the resulting trade will be for 1 mini lot.

The stop-loss level and take-profit level (the operation and importance of the stop loss are explained at a later stage) are grayed out because this is a market order. In the part called "Type," we determine if the trade will be executed instantly through what is called a *market order* or whether it will be executed at a certain price that you specify (if it becomes available)—something that is called a *pending* or *limit order.* We also see the display of the now-familiar bid/ask prices, with two corresponding buttons below them. When you press the Sell button, the order is executed using the bid price, whereas when you press the Buy button, the order is executed at the ask price. When the brokerage firm gives you access to a trading platform, it lets you pick the number of contracts you wish to trade. If you have enough collateral (or enough *margin*), the broker will let you enter into the trade you want.

FIGURE 4-2 Order Window

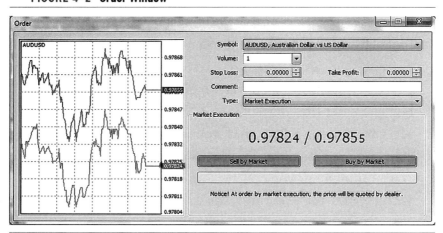

SAMPLE TRADE

In our particular example, we request a Sell AUDUSD order at 0.97824 (Figure 4-2). Since this is a market order, we are placed in a trade at the first available price, which in our case happens to be 0.97828, about the price we requested. The cost for this trade is –$32 (3.2 pips in spread × $10 each pip × 1 standard lot). To let you enter into this trade for AUD 100,000 units, the broker requires a margin of US$1,956.56.[2] The amount of *required margin* does not become the property of the broker; it is only held in reserve. If you close the trade profitably, the margin amount plus a trading gain is returned to your account. If there was a trading loss, the margin minus the trading loss is returned.

> **KEY CONCEPT:** Too many beginner traders pay a high price for failing to grasp the relationship between trade size and margin required. By leaving little free margin available, the inexperienced trader draws dangerously close to a margin call situation and puts at risk not just the margined amount but the whole account.

In my view, brokers should do more to explain to new traders what is a prudent trade-size level based on the account size. The example in Figure 4-2 (buying 1 standard lot in a US$5,000 account) is above what I consider prudent, but we are using it here to illustrate the point. In Figure 4-3, we can see trade information such as the trade execution price when we started the trade (in GMT, or Greenwich

FIGURE 4-3 Sample FX Trade: SELL AUDUSD

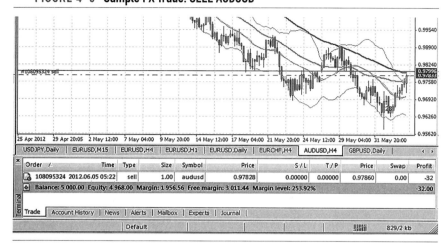

Mean Time) and the *floating* profit (loss). We also see a floating loss of –32, which should be understood as –3.2 pips.

It so happens that this trade was profitable. When the trade reaches a net profit of about 25 pips, I decided to close the trade. To do this, I highlighted the open trade in the Terminal section and pressed the right button of the mouse. From the options available, I selected Close Trade. A new pop-up window opened up (Figure 4-4). In the section below the Sell and Buy buttons, I pressed the Close button.

To evaluate the result of our trade, we look at the Terminal section and click on the Account History tab (Figure 4-5). As we look at the trade information—open time of 2012.06.05 05:22 and close time of 2012.06.05 07:25—we see that in a period of two hours and three minutes, the trade captured $263 (net of $32 in spread costs), a 5.3 percent net profit on a $5,000 account.

FIGURE 4-4 Closing a Trade

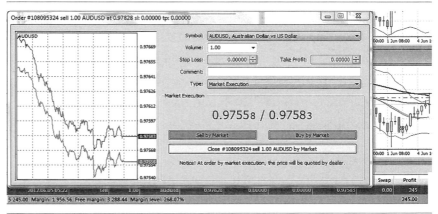

FIGURE 4-5 Account History Window

Order	Time	Type	Size	Symbol	Price	S/L	T/P	Time ⊤	Price	Swap	Profit
108095324	2012.06.05 05:22	sell	1.00	audusd	0.97828	0.00000	0.00000	2012.06.05 07:25	0.97565	0.00	263.00
108095250	2012.06.05 05:12	balance								Deposit	5 000.00
Profit/Loss: 263.00 Credit: 0.00 Deposit: 5 000.00 Withdrawal: 0.00											5 263.00

Trade | Account History | News | Alerts | Mailbox | Experts | Journal |

To recap, we entered into an AUDUSD trade with a contract size equivalent to 100,000 Australian dollars, putting a
margin (collateral) of $1,956.56 from our $5,000 account. The
broker allowed us to *leverage* a 2 percent margin amount into
a contract 50 times the size of our collateral. We achieved the
profit because we sold AUDUSD and the price fell below our
entry point. We closed the trade 29.5 pips below the entry
point, but we netted 26.3 pips after deducting the 3 pips in
the AUDUSD spread to get into the trade.

Some might say that this was a good trade. A 5.3 percent return in two hours shows us the good, generous side of forex trading. Of course, without taking precautions, the same power of forex trading has a habit of reaching deep into the pockets of undisciplined traders. Some of these precautions include things such as having a sensible trade size and using a stop loss to limit the risk of loss.

LEVERAGE AND MARGIN LEVEL EXPLAINED

I hope that by now you are starting to see how trading margin is linked to trade size and to individual currency pairs. I would also like you to think of the term *leverage* as a multiplier of your capital. The lower the leverage level (or multiplier), the bigger the amount of capital you need to deposit in your trading account. A high leverage level allows the holder of a small account to trade a large contract size. The bigger the contract size, the bigger the potential gain or loss is.

One of the tricks for achieving the highest potential gain with the capital we have available is to qualify for the highest leverage level but use only a small percentage of it (that is, use smaller trade sizes). It's like qualifying for a $200,000 line of credit but using only $2,000 of it on a regular basis. But just like having a credit card with a high line of credit, it requires discipline to use only what we can pay at the end of the month.

So if having a high leverage level is like qualifying for a large credit line, what is margin required? *Margin required*

TABLE 4-1 Leverage and Margin Required When the
U.S. Dollar Is the Base Currency

CONTRACT NAME	MARGIN REQUIRED (YOUR COLLATERAL)	CONTRACT SIZE (IN US$)	MARGIN LEVEL (IN PERCENTAGE)	LEVERAGE LEVEL
1 micro lot	$20.00	$1,000	2.0%	50:1
1 mini lot	$200.00	$10,000	2.0%	50:1
1 standard lot	$2,000.00	$100,000	2.0%	50:1

is the amount you are borrowing from that credit line. You probably pay interest on what you are buying on credit. Likewise, it makes sense to know how margin required is calculated.

The margin required is calculated differently depending on the currency pair that we are trading. For currency pairs in which the U.S. dollar is the base currency (USDJPY, USDCHF, USDCAD, and so on), Table 4-1 illustrates how the margin is calculated for different contract sizes.

Until 2010, the most common leverage level used to be 100:1 for standard accounts and 200:1 for mini and micro accounts.[3] Since then, forex traders in the United States have had to get used to a maximum leverage level of 50:1 (that is, a 2.0 percent margin level). Essentially, this has meant that we traders have had to either deposit more money in our accounts than we did prior to 2010 or keep the same amount of money we had and place trades that are half or a fourth of what they used to be. Even so, the leverage for trading forex is the highest offered to U.S. retail traders—more so than the rates offered in stock, futures, or options trading.

TABLE 4-2 Leverage and Margin Required When the
U.S. Dollar Is the Quote Currency

CURRENCY PAIR	SAMPLE PRICE	MARGIN REQUIRED (IN US$)	CONTRACT SIZE: 1 STANDARD LOT	LEVERAGE LEVEL
EURUSD	1.5534	$3,106.80	EUR 100,000	50:1
EURUSD	1.1527	$2,305.40	EUR 100,000	50:1
GBPUSD	1.6536	$3,307.20	GBP 100,000	50:1
GBPUSD	1.3598	$2,719.60	GBP 100,000	50:1
AUDUSD	0.9726	$1,945.20	AUD 100,000	50:1
NZDUSD	0.6960	$1,392.00	NZD 100,000	50:1

From Table 4-2, we can appreciate how pairs in which the U.S. dollar is the quote currency (EURUSD, GBPUSD, and so on) may require us to post more margin than we saw in Table 4-1. Please also note that the amount that we need for margin changes with the price of the currency pair—we are required to post less margin when EURUSD has a lower price than when it has a higher price.

I don't expect anyone to fully comprehend all of this margin discussion the first time she reads it. I encourage you to read it a few times. Ultimately, I would like you to feel uncomfortable when you are using too much of your available margin. The quickest way to know how much leverage you are using at any given time is to look at the margin level.

THE MARGIN CALL

One of the saddest things I've had to do is to explain to someone (even to money managers) how his account blew up because, knowingly or unknowingly, he got too close to a margin call. How does a margin call get activated while trading forex? Simply put, margin calls happen for two reasons:

1. A person places too big a trade for the size of an account.
2. The trader refuses to close a losing trade before the loss becomes critically large.

KEY CONCEPT: Most forex brokers have systems that automatically trigger a margin call when the margin level reaches 50 percent. At a margin level of 100 percent, most brokers prevent you from placing any new trades. A person can increase the margin level by simply closing open trades (partial close or full close).

At a margin level of 50 percent, the equity of an account has become half as large as the margin required to keep whatever trades are open.

Let's test your knowledge of the concepts we covered in this chapter with the following example. Each of two traders has a US$5,000 trading account balance and one open trade. Neither of them has set a stop loss.

- Trader A bought 1.0 standard lot of AUDUSD (margin required of US$1,956.56) and has a margin level of 254 percent.
- Trader B bought 1.7 mini lots of AUDUSD (margin required of US$332.62) and has a margin level of 1,503 percent.

The two of them go to bed, and while they are asleep, the prime minister of Australia is killed in a terrorist car bomb attack. Markets are in turmoil. By the time the traders wake up to check on their respective open trades, the Aussie has plummeted 450 pips, only to rise back up 200 pips. Which of the two trading accounts (if either) survived this highly volatile environment? Here is how we do the math on this scenario:

> *Trader A.* By the time AUDUSD dropped 405 pips, the equity of Trader A had plummeted from $5,000 to $950 (the $4,050 drop is calculated thus: 405 × $10 pip value × 1 standard lot). At US$950, the margin level for this account becomes 49 percent. The brokerage firm's system triggers a margin call that closes the one open trade, and the loss of approximately US$4,050 is realized. The ending balance is about US$950.

> *Trader B.* Even with a drop of 450 pips, the equity of Trader B dropped temporarily in value by US$765. The math for this drop is: –450 pips × 1.7 mini lots × $1 pip value. After the Aussie recovered 200 pips, the open trade of Trader B shows a US$425 floating loss (equity of US$4,575, margin level of 1,375 percent).

Hopefully your eyes are more open with regard to the use of margin: being stingy with the use of margin means sleeping better at night. Just for the fun of it, suppose both traders in our example had *sold* AUDUSD instead of buying it. Trader A would have awakened to find an open profit of US$2,500 (margin level 383 percent), and Trader B would have an open profit of US$425 (margin level of 1,631 percent).

Technical Analysis

My most memorable lesson about road signs came while I was riding a bike in Nancy, a city in the Lorraine region of eastern France. This particular morning, I was riding my bike downhill, and I had reached a speed of approximately 35 mph. To my surprise, all the cars to my left began to slow down. I did not see any reason why they were doing so. Of course, I kept going fast—until a vehicle came out of an intersection I was about to cross. I remember slamming on the brakes late, crashing into the side of this car, flying over the hood, and landing ungracefully on the pavement. I was very fortunate; I came away with only a few bruises and a *heightened* appreciation for road signs.

Now that you are familiar with the trading platform and how to enter a trade, you will naturally need to learn to recognize the road signs that forex traders follow. The study of charts, or technical analysis, is what tells forex drivers when to get into a trade and, just as important, when they should *not* trade.

This chapter will illustrate some of the most basic technical analysis principles that will guide your trading: candlestick charts, support and resistance lines, and basic technical indicators. I strongly encourage you to read books and take video courses that are dedicated exclusively to teaching technical analysis techniques. This chapter will merely be a primer, and those who are not trading novices can safely skip to the next chapter.

The price of a currency pair can be displayed in multiple ways: as bar charts, candlestick charts, or line charts (Figure 5-1). Today, candlestick charts are the most popular way to conduct technical studies, although many old-school traders prefer bar charts.

Candlestick analysis has been around for centuries; it had its origin among rice traders in Japan. This *Eastern* form of technical analysis was not known in the Western world until some of the original Japanese texts were translated. Steve Nison (pronounced "Nee-son"), a prominent technical analysis guru, can be credited with having made candlestick analysis widely adopted in North America and Europe.

In candlestick charts, changes in currency prices are contained within the shape of candles, or, more precisely, candlesticks. Each candlestick may give clues that predict the future direction of currency prices. The formation of several candlesticks also may shed light on both the directions of price trends and their intensity. In short, learning to understand candlestick formations is as critical as interpreting road signs.

FIGURE 5-1 **Types of Charts**

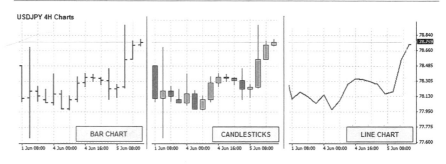

We see in Figure 5-2 that the rectangular part of a candlestick is called the *real body*. Most trading platforms allow users to customize real body colors. In Figure 5-2, we see a white candle and a black candle. We will assume that the candles we are looking at are 1-hour candles.[1] The candle on the left opens at minute 00:00, for example, and closes one hour later at 01:00. The color of the real body in a candle will depend on the answer to this question: was the close price higher, lower, or the same as the candle open price? The white candlestick is what we would call a *bullish candle*: the close price was higher than the open price. The black candlestick in the picture is a *bearish candle*: the close price was below the open price.

Why use the terms *bullish* and *bearish*? A bull charges its prey with a lifting motion of its horns (from low to high), whereas when a bear attacks, it lowers its paws upon the prey (from high to low).

FIGURE 5-2 Candlestick Chart Explained

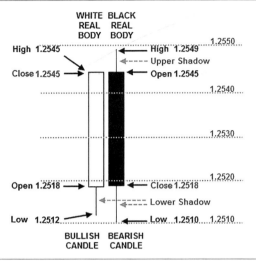

When the open and close prices are the same, the real body is just a black horizontal line with vertical *upper* and *lower shadow* sticks. Thus, the real body displays the open and close prices, while the upper and lower shadows deal with how high or low the price traded during the hour. Sometimes the close price may be the highest or lowest price traded. Thus, sometimes there isn't an upper or lower shadow in a given candle.

What I hope you can come to appreciate about candlestick charting is that candlestick patterns are a bit of a science. Gaining the right reading of these patterns will come with time, as you train your eye by trading often and by increasing your knowledge of candlesticks. I strongly recommend that you visit www.candlecharts.com to further your learning in this area.

CHART PATTERNS

Just about every trader has a theory concerning the patterns that dictate the movements of a security. Of course, if someone is truly right, she should be able to profit from this kind of knowledge. Some people say that securities follow historical cycles, others believe that they are random in nature, and still others say that they are ruled by technical and fundamental factors. It is healthy to look at patterns as probabilities, not certainties. Beware of any person who claims that he can predict with accuracy what currency prices will do *all the time*. However, many people have learned to predict *short-term currency price movements* based on patterns and probabilities. There are even some pattern recognition tools, such as the one found in www.autochartist.com, that will automatically identify the patterns seen in Figure 5-3. The black line within each pattern represents the behavior of currency prices.

There are also patterns that tell us that the trend paused and then continued in the previous direction (continuation patterns), turned around (reversal patterns), or showed a combination of continuation and reversal patterns (Figure 5-4).

SUPPORT AND RESISTANCE LINES

The basic price patterns that we just touched on can be drawn manually using what we call *support* and *resistance* lines. It is not far-fetched to say that currency prices often behave like bouncy balls, hitting floors and ceilings. The floor or low point of a price bounce is called *support*, while the ceiling or high point of the bounce is called *resistance*. The horizontal

FIGURE 5-3 Popular Chart Patterns

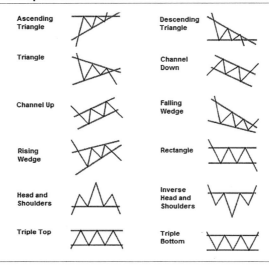

Source: Autochartist.com

FIGURE 5-4 Trend Continuation and Reversal

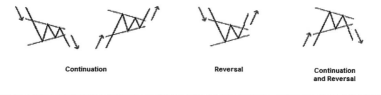

Continuation   Reversal   Continuation and Reversal

Source: Autochartist.com

lines seen in Figure 5-5 form a support line at EURCHF 1.20495 and a resistance line at approximately 1.2060.

For the major part of the six-day period depicted in the chart, EURCHF (euro-swissie) traded within a very tight 11-pip range before it "broke out" to the upside on March 13. Remember that the daily trading range of the euro-dollar is

FIGURE 5-5 Support and Resistance Lines, EURCHF 1-Hour Chart

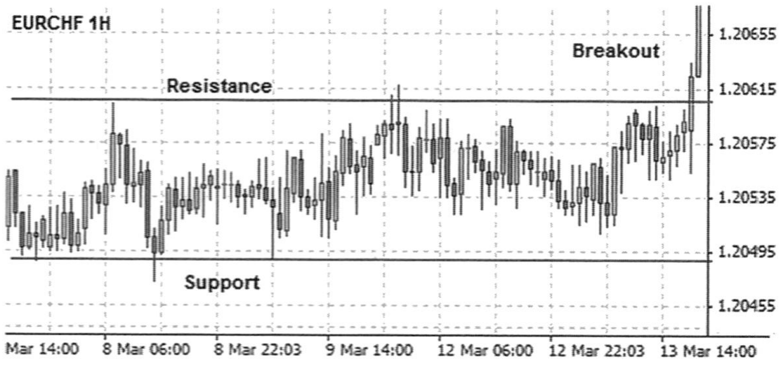

Note: Each candle in the chart represents 1 hour.

something like 110 to 120 pips, so in Figure 5-5, we could say that the swissie was (for a short period) *pegged* to the euro. With a trading range this tight, I would not have seen much value in trading this pair.

The breakout seen in Figure 5-5 can be defined as the point when the price exits a pattern formation abruptly. The longer a trend is in place, the stronger the breakout is. Shrewd traders follow the trend but are also prepared for eventual breakouts and trend reversals. A fine example of how to follow the trend can be seen in Figure 5-6. In this daily chart of the EURUSD, prices fell a very sharp 12 percent in 10 weeks, from 1.4140 to 1.2575, while staying in a *channel* down. The opportunity for someone who trades using the daily chart could be to:

- *Sell* EURUSD as the price approaches within 20 pips of the channel resistance line, set a stop loss 35 pips above the resistance line, and set the profit target 30 pips above the support line.

- *Buy* EURUSD as the price approaches within 20 pips of the channel support line, set a stop loss 35 pips below the support line, and set the profit target at the midpoint of the channel.

Note how EURUSD prices bounce (circles) against these support and resistance lines multiple times. Anyone who has been around trading knows that this rate of decline (12 percent in 10 weeks) can't last for long. The stop loss is a way to protect the trader when prices break out of the descending channel. Sure enough, this trend ended on January 18, when the daily candle close happened above the resistance line *and* subsequent candles closed above the resistance line.

FIGURE 5-6 Support and Resistance Lines and Reversal, EURUSD Daily Chart

Note: Each candle represents 1 day.

—————————— SELF-QUIZ ——————————

Let's help a fellow trader do some math. On January 18, he saw an opportunity to *sell* one standard lot of EURUSD at 1.2800, and he took it. He was so sure that the euro would fall back within the channel down that he didn't use a stop loss. He thinks that the floating loss showing on his platform is too big and faulty. Help him calculate his floating loss as EURUSD reaches 1.3200 and what would have happened if he had capped the loss at 1.2835 (1.2800 resistance line plus 35 pips).

Answer:

- Loss with the stop loss at 1.2835: $10 pip value × −35 pips × 1 standard lot = −$350
- Floating loss once it reaches 1.3200: $10 × −400 pips × 1 = −$4,000

DRAWING SUPPORT AND RESISTANCE LINES

When you create a new chart, the support and resistance lines will not appear automatically; you need to learn how to identify and draw your own support and resistance lines. These lines do not always have to be perfectly symmetrical. Of course, there are many technical analysts on major forex websites that will be more than happy to share with you the reader what they perceive to be important support and resistance levels. If you believe the analyst is any good, you can simply copy those support and resistance lines onto your charts.

One good way to know where to draw a support line is by uniting several of the lowest prices seen on the chart.

Likewise, a resistance line can be drawn by uniting several of the highest prices (peaks). The more bounces there are along a support or resistance line, the more important the pattern formation becomes.

Basic Technical Indicators

Forex traders use technical indicators to identify the trend direction, trend opportunities, and the optimal prices at which to enter and exit a trade.

There are dozens of technical indicators that are included in most trading platforms, including MACD, stochastic oscillator, Bollinger bands, and Fibonacci retracement. There are also platforms that allow users to develop their own (custom) indicators.

Over time, you will master a number of technical indicators that you find are most useful to you. The purpose of this book is to explore some in more detail than others. We next explore Fibonacci studies.

Fibonacci Studies

There is an interesting story behind the Fibonacci name and its application to trading. Leonardo Pisano (c. 1170–1250), also known as Fibonacci, was a brilliant Italian mathematician who discovered a unique numeric sequence that bears his name. This sequence starts with 0 and 1, and each subsequent number is the sum of the previous two numbers. Thus, the sequence begins 0, 1, 1, 2, 3, 5, 8, 13, 21, 34, 55, 89, 144, 233, 377, 610, and so on. The higher up you go in the sequence, the closer two consecutive Fibonacci numbers divided by each other will approach what is known as the *golden ratio*. This special ratio can be shown in multiple ways—1:1.618 or 0.618:1 or 61.8 percent.

$$0 + 1 = \mathbf{1} \qquad 1 + 1 = \mathbf{2} \qquad 1 + 2 = \mathbf{3}$$
$$2 + 3 = \mathbf{5} \qquad 3 + 5 = \mathbf{8} \qquad 5 + 8 = \mathbf{13}$$
$$8 + 13 = \mathbf{21} \qquad 13 + 21 = \mathbf{34} \qquad 21 + 34 = \mathbf{55}$$

$$\mathbf{89/144} = 0.6180 \qquad\qquad \mathbf{144/233} = 0.6180$$
$$\mathbf{233/377} = 0.6180 \qquad\qquad \mathbf{377/610} = 0.6180$$

The golden ratio predated the Fibonacci sequence and was widely adopted in art, architecture, and music. Experts in science and nature have also identified the golden ratio in nature. Since there are so many examples of the golden ratio and the Fibonacci sequence in many areas of life, it found its way into technical analysis too! Traders use *key Fibonacci ratios* (23.6 percent, 38.2 percent, 50.0 percent, 61.8 percent, and 76.4 percent). The trading platform has tools that automatically calculate these ratios in a chart. There are so-called Fibonacci retracements, Fibonacci extensions, and Fibonacci fans and arcs. Since there is a great deal that could be written about these different aspects of Fibonacci studies, I will limit this discussion to Fibonacci retracements.

KEY CONCEPT: The theory around Fibonacci retracements is that currency prices tend to use the key Fibonacci ratios as natural support and resistance lines. So, if you know where Fibonacci ratios are located within a chart, you have one more way to analyze the behavior of price movements and can position your trade in the right direction and with the right stop-loss/take-profit levels.

Fibonacci *retracements* get their name from the observation that currency prices routinely *retrace* their steps. Retracing after a price rally means that prices start to fall, and retracing after a price drop means that prices start to rise again. So, how do we draw Fibonacci retracements within the MT4 platform?

1. Identify *swing high* and *swing low* points. A swing high is a candlestick with at least two lower highs on both the left and right of it. A swing low is the mirror image, a candlestick with at least two higher lows on both the left and the right of it.
2. Identify whether the market is in an uptrend or a downtrend.

During a downtrend, prices are moving generally lower but reach a point where they start rising somewhat. They then retrace to resistance lines, which may be at or close to Fibonacci levels. In this scenario, traders tend to place very short-term sell orders when prices touch the 38.2 percent or 50.0 percent Fibonacci levels. Likewise, they may place buy

FIGURE 5-7 Fibonacci Downtrend Reversal, EURUSD Daily Chart

Note: Each candle represents 1 day.

orders as the price approaches the 23.6 percent Fibonacci level.

To replicate a chart like the one in Figure 5-7, you would:

1. Identify the downtrend pattern for a currency.
2. Click on the Fibonacci icon on the MT4 platform.
3. Click on the swing high and swing low points you identified (click on the swing high first).

During an uptrend, prices are moving generally higher but reach a point at which they fall somewhat. Prices are said to be retracing to find support, and this support line could be a Fibonacci level. During an uptrend, traders tend to

FIGURE 5-8 Fibonacci Uptrend Reversal, AUDUSD Daily Chart

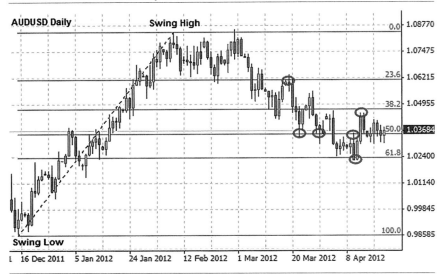

Note: Each candle represents 1 day.

place very short-term buy orders when prices fall to certain Fibonacci levels, like 38.2 percent, 50 percent, and particularly 61.8 percent. The circles in Figures 5-7 and 5-8 show the high level of activity (price bouncing) around the Fibonacci levels.

To recreate an uptrend Fibonacci reversal, you would follow steps similar to those for the downtrend, *except* that you'd click on the swing low point first and then on the swing high point.

KEY CONCEPT: It is likely that the first few times you draw Fibonacci retracements, you might choose swing highs and lows that are not very relevant. This is OK. The more you use the Fibonacci tool, the more you will become familiar with the levels that are most relevant to the market.

I should state once more that this is a very light overview of selected major technical analysis methods that are followed by vast numbers of traders. My goal at this point is to provide you with sufficient technical analysis background to understand the trading strategy that I will discuss more deeply in the upcoming chapters.

Fundamental Analysis

Fundamental analysis looks at various types of topics, such as rates of inflation, interest rates, and rates of economic growth, and ranks countries based on these "fundamental" rates. The astute forex trader will seek to understand the context, or big picture, that is driving currencies up or down. Fundamental analysis tells us the overall direction of a currency based on many factors, while technical analysis tells us when is the best time to buy or sell a particular currency. The two work hand in hand.

There is a great deal to be said about fundamental analysis, so I've compiled the key factors that I think are most important to help the reader get a handle on this type of analysis.

Trading the News

The release of major economic news often includes surprises that change important market expectations. At least for a few minutes, a release can generate wild price swings up and down (volatility), something that makes trading during these periods unsuitable for beginners and for the faint of heart. Think of the price volatility surrounding important economic announcements as having two levels of intensity. The first, very intense wave of volatility lasts for up to the first 15 minutes following the data release. The second wave starts when the first leaves off and lasts one to three hours. How do you know when the second wave has started? The spreads will return to normal. During the first phase, spreads on EURUSD will shoot up briefly from 2 pips or less to 5, 10, or 15 pips. Spreads on other currencies will shoot up even higher.

These major economic announcements often trigger currency trend reversals and propel currency prices past major support and resistance levels. Often the volatility will trigger large pending orders, such as hedges around big figures and sitting breakout orders. Institutional bank traders, reluctant corporate treasurers, and thrill-seeking retail traders all converge and trade during these crazy periods.

Trading the news carries misunderstood risks. I've heard many retail traders claim that they were scammed out of an order when they requested it at a certain price but got something completely different. "The broker didn't honor the price" is a frequent claim.

To shed some light on what's really going on, I will compare trading the news to getting into the hottest nightclub in a major city. The bouncer stands at the door, and he makes night revelers form a line. If there's room in the establishment, the bouncer will be told, and he will let someone in.

Now let's look at what happens to price availability when important economic news is released. A few minutes before the release, there is a major drop in liquidity. It's as if the invisible hand of the market had said, "No more bets, thank you," but you still see a few wild mini jumps in price on the trading platform. It would be a mistake to think that you can trade on the prices shown in those mini jumps.

> **KEY CONCEPT:** Here lies the error that many "news traders"
> make: they assume that just because a price appeared (how-
> ever briefly) on their trading platform, it gives them a right to
> execute their trade at that price.

A trader who wants to trade at a price he sees on the platform right before or right after an economic announcement is as misguided as a tourist getting off a cab at New York's 1 Oak at 11 p.m. on Friday and expecting to waltz right in. And who could blame him? He did see a web article saying that it was a cool hangout. The sanitized version of what the bouncer would tell him would be: "Buddy, it doesn't work like that. Do you see the end of this line? Good luck."

Let me restate this. Liquidity, the precious lifeblood of trading, *dries up* during the crazed moments before and after an economic announcement. It's as if the nightclub reaches the quota of people established by the city's building code.

Let's say the June U.S. nonfarm payroll number is announced, and it was good for stock markets and the euro.

You hurry and put in a market order to buy EURUSD at the 1.3274 price you see in your screen. The problem is that the price of 1.3274 may have been available because one of your broker's liquidity banks offered $2 million at that price. But alas, the broker gets $45 million worth of demand at 1.3274 for that lonely $2 million. It seems that great minds think alike, and your buy order had plenty of company. So what does the broker's automated matching system do? Like the good bouncer it is, it fills the $2 million with whoever was in line first. It then looks for the next EURUSD selling price available to fill the remaining $43 million worth of buy requests. If that next matching price is 1.3299, then that's the price your market order will get filled at.[1] It would be also wrong to assume that a pending order will do better than a market order. Pending orders also form a queue, and prices may gap over the limit order price.

> **KEY CONCEPT:** It is extremely difficult to make money during the first wave of volatility following a news announcement. You pay a wide spread to get into the trade, and there is no guarantee that you will get the fill you are looking to get on the trade. If you must trade at all during this period, try to do so during the second wave of volatility as liquidity and spreads return to normal.

There are, of course, clever solutions available to help retail traders get first in line during news announcements. They work relatively well. The problem, however, is that the broker's welcome mat will be rolled up very quickly and the person using such a system will become persona non grata. Pretty soon you will run out of brokers and have to start sending your money to offshore brokers, which can lead to other kinds of problems—like trying to withdraw your money. The key lesson about trading the news is to do it as a last resort during the second wave of volatility and to have a healthy respect for the changes in liquidity that take place immediately before and after these events.

Major economic announcements

Next, I would like to identify which are the major events to look for (Table 6-1). The rating column represents the importance that I have measured for each event relative to the top three (G3) currency pairs: the U.S. dollar, the euro, and the yen.

The first week of the month is generally quite volatile, with the Bank of Australia interest-rate announcement on Tuesday, the U.S. ADP labor number (an increasingly important preview of U.S. nonfarm payrolls) on Wednesday, the U.K. and European official bank rate on Thursday, and the U.S. nonfarm payrolls and U.S. unemployment rate on Friday. In addition to economic announcements, there are other types of news releases that can also affect currency markets significantly:

- Election and referendum results
- Corporate earnings of major companies, such as stocks of Cisco, Apple, and banks

TABLE 6-1 Main Economic Announcements

ECONOMIC ANNOUNCEMENT	COUNTRY
Nonfarm payrolls/employment data	United States
Federal Open Market Committee (FOMC) announcement	United States
Minimum bid rate/ECB press conference	European Union
Consumer Price Index (CPI)	United States
Speech by central bank president	United States, European Union, United Kingdom
Trade balance	United States
Gross domestic product	United States, European Union, United Kingdom
Retail sales	United States, United Kingdom
Official bank rate	United Kingdom, Australia, Canada, Switzerland
Tankan Large Manufacturers Index	Japan
Consumer Prices Index (CPI)	EU, U.K., AU, CA, CH
Overnight call rate/Bank of Japan press conference	Japan
German IFO business climate	European Union

RELEVANCE	NOTES	RATING
It measures job creation in the United States, which is seen as a forecast of future U.S. expenditures	First Friday of the month	10
The U.S. Federal Reserve reveals changes in U.S. interest rates	Two-day meeting, eight times per year	10
The European Central Bank announces the key bank rate	First Thursday of the month	7
It tells us the rate of inflation or deflation at the consumer level	Monthly	6
Always important; the market looks for clues to future interest-rate policy and other policy steps to intervene in capital markets.	Ben Bernanke (United States), Mervyn King (United Kingdom), Mario Draghi (European Union)	5
Reveals imbalances in U.S. trade with China and the rest of the world	Monthly	5
The economy's rate of growth is always important	The advanced rate is the most important	4
Retail purchases are the engine of the U.S. and U.K. economies	Monthly	4
The central banks of the United Kingdom, Australia, Switzerland, and Canada announce the key bank lending rate	Very important for GBP, AUD, CHF, and CAD, respectively	3
Key indicator of Japan's manufacturing sector	Quarterly	3
The consumer price index for the Eurozone, U.K., Australia, Canada and Switzerland show whether changes in official bank rates may need to go up or down.	Very important for GBP, AUD, CAD respectively	3
The Bank of Japan announces the key bank rate	Not as volatile since 0% rate policy started	2
Shows the level of confidence of German businesses in the economy	Monthly	2

- Major political events: wars, military or terrorist attacks, warlike rhetoric
- The bankruptcy of a major market participant (Refco, Long-Term Capital Management, Lehman Brothers, MF Global)
- Sovereign debt auction results (when governments borrow private funds)
- Natural or human-made disasters: tsunamis, nuclear accidents, droughts, floods, major earthquakes in sensitive areas (major financial centers, oil-producing areas, and so on)
- Prices of commodities (crude oil, copper, precious metals) and threats of commodities disruption
- Government policies: deficit spending, trade restrictions, and so on

Along with all the things in the previous list, major economic events have an impact on currency prices. Currencies become a way for global markets to make adjustments. If the United States suffers from trade deficits with other nations, the invisible hand of the markets will tend to weaken the U.S. dollar. Once the U.S. dollar weakens, U.S. manufacturers will increase their exports and the U.S. trade deficit should become smaller and eventually disappear. As the trade balance improves, the dollar would also gain strength.

As a matter of principle, currency markets tend to weaken the currencies of countries that

- Borrow too much—a way for the markets to tell them to change this behavior

- Have large trade deficits—a way for the markets to tell them to export more and import less
- Pay low interest rates on deposits—money flows to where it can achieve the highest return
- Have low rates of economic growth—without growth, countries have less means to pay their debts
- Have high unemployment rates—a weak labor market leads to lower economic growth and lower future values for assets like homes and businesses; markets signal to the country that it needs to export more or change its labor laws so that employers are more likely to hire people
- Engage in wars—money that is going to fund wars is money that is not going to productive uses of capital

Here is an uncomfortable question: what happens if a country's currency cannot be adjusted by global markets?

Answer: The problems are not resolved; they get worse and have more explosive outcomes.

KEY CONCEPT: In a world of freely floating currencies, currency markets have a way to adjust prices to achieve a balance between the supply and the demand of global goods, services, and investments. As we analyze economic fundamentals, however, we must quickly come to grips with the fact that we don't live in a world in which all nations play by the same rules (or play fair with one another, for that matter).

In fact, not all major currencies float freely. China is the prime example of a very important country (the second-largest economy in the world) that keeps its currency—the yuan or renminbi—arbitrarily low relative to the U.S. dollar. This policy benefits Chinese factories at the expense of U.S. factories. The United States also plays by self-serving sets of rules. It benefits greatly from a decision dating back to the early 1940s in which the U.S. dollar was essentially named the main global currency for commerce and exchange. Thus, changes in U.S. monetary policy affect the whole world, not just the United States.

MAJOR FOREX THEMES: THE U.S. DOLLAR

I can understand why many people who feel that the United States is headed in the wrong direction would be eager to sell the U.S. dollar against other currencies. What I hope you can come to understand is that while you may have your own opinion about what the U.S. dollar is worth, you have to respect even more what the market says it is worth.

Maybe you are looking at the value of the U.S. dollar from the perspective that the United States has a massive public debt and has a president who does not belong to your political party. Meanwhile, the global markets are saying: "Yes, the U.S. debt is a problem, but other countries have it as bad or worse, *and* the United States is the only place large enough and with the right labor laws, right legal protections, and so on to put our cash to productive use."

In practical terms, if all we do when we trade is sell the U.S. dollar, we will get creamed before too long. We need to be able to buy the U.S. dollar when our technical analysis *and* our fundamental analysis say so. One of the few times the U.S. dollar was weakening against the euro and other currencies came during the 2007 to 2008 subprime crisis and the start of the credit crisis. The world saw Europe as a safer bet, largely immune from U.S. problems. But even during this period, any time the world heard something frightening and ran for cover, it bought U.S. Treasury securities. What currency benefited from that purchase? Yes, the U.S. dollar.

My advice to you is to check at the door your strong views on what currency should be strong, sit down to trade with an open mind, and let the charts and fundamental indicators tell you what currency is best to buy or sell. One more word of advice is to largely ignore news headlines that say that the euro or yen gained against the U.S. dollar (or vice versa). News headlines have a way of rattling the inexperienced but are generally meant to grab attention. By the time a headline stating that the euro gained 1 percent against the dollar comes out, the dollar is most likely already taking most of that 1 percent back.

MAJOR FOREX THEMES: THE DEBT CRISIS

The debt crisis was triggered in the United States in 2008 with the bankruptcy of Lehman Brothers and the forced merger of several other important financial firms (Bear Stearns,

Merrill Lynch, Wachovia, and Washington Mutual). The crisis got put on hold in the United States through aggressive action by the Federal Reserve. Some of these measures, called quantitative easing (rounds one and two; now there is talk of round three), boosted U.S. stock markets and cut interest rates to near zero.

EUROPE

The problems, however, were exported to Iceland, Greece, Ireland, Portugal, Greece again, and Italy, and they are now threatening Spain and every other European country that is unwilling to be accountable for its public finances. Iceland essentially decided to take care of its own rather than to pay outside creditors—ironically, it is now experiencing robust growth and is in a better financial situation to start honoring previous financial obligations.

The road that European leaders have taken since December 2009 to help Greece, Ireland, Portugal, and Spain, however, has been more painful than what Iceland did. If Europe can be compared to a family, big brother Germany told party-loving kid sister Greece: I will pay your huge monthly payments for two years if you agree to take this flip phone and sell your iPhone 4S, sell everything inside your closet that has a known brand name, trade that leased BMW M6 parked in front of your house for a two-door Yugo, and give me the money you make so that I may manage it. Kicking and screaming, Greece agreed to the terms. Jet-set-loving brother Spain and easygoing sister Italy saw the writing on the wall and started selling off their villas by the beach. In other words, the recipe for

Europe so far has been to tighten its belt and show that Europe honors most of its debt commitments and cuts most wasteful expenses. Big brother Germany now insists that all members of the family sign a blood pact (constitutional amendment) to make it illegal to spend more than what each family member has in the bank. The family is going along, but you never know what could happen a year from now. Rumor has it that there will be a north-south split.

Why is belt tightening the only way out of the problem that Europe can see? The reasons are complex, but they essentially boil down to the fact that these indebted countries use the same currency, the euro. In olden days, global markets would have seen the debt problems of Greece and solved them by weakening the Greek drachma. A weak drachma would have led to a tourism and real estate bonanza in Greece, eventually causing the drachma to appreciate against other currencies. Today, however, none of the 17 eurozone nations (including Greece) can take that route because the euro that unites them happens to be quite strong—thanks in large measure to Germany. I should mention that we Americans love to speculate about an imminent European split, but Europe has a long history that values continental unity more deeply than we can see on the surface. There are strong forces that keep Europe together.

UNITED STATES

The debt problems are concentrated in three places: Europe, the United States, and Japan. The day of reckoning for the United States is not far off, maybe in 2013 or 2014. Credit rating agencies have already taken the unprecedented step of lowering the credit rating of the United States one notch down from AAA. The lower credit rating means that the interest payments on the large U.S. public debt will go higher. More downgrades could take place if the U.S. Congress and the president (Obama or Romney) don't agree to major cuts to make the U.S. federal government better able to live within its means.

There is very likely an impasse ahead if Democrats retain the White House. Obama wants to raise taxes on the rich, while Republicans are adamantly opposed to raising taxes. The Republicans' solution is to dramatically cut the size of the government, cut taxes, and trust that the economy will grow robustly and thus bring in enough revenues to pay down the debt. The two parties stand far apart on this important issue, something that could invite a further downgrade of U.S. debt and a very volatile environment for trading currencies—which is a good thing.

JAPAN

Japan is the most indebted country by many measures, but it is not yet under as much pressure to get its debt problems under control as the United States and Europe are. Japan's large advantage is that the vast majority of Japanese debt is held by Japanese citizens. Unlike foreign debtholders, Japanese debtholders are not likely to "dump" public debt because they are in the same boat as the government is.

The reason Japan finds itself in this fix is that it suffered vicious real estate and stock market crashes in the 1990s.

These events triggered a steady fall in consumer prices over the past 10 to 12 years, something known as deflation. Economic growth is achieved when prices increase from year to year, but the absence of price growth is leading Japan to experience a rise in its debt burden. Japan's low birthrate and the increasing longevity of its citizens will only compound the debt problem. The inability of Japanese governments to tackle these long-term problems is also a major issue. The day of reckoning in Japan over its debt is not imminent, but it will come. Think of the debt problems facing the world as Europe causing currency volatility today, the United States causing it tomorrow, and Japan causing it the day after tomorrow.

MAJOR FOREX THEMES: INTEREST AND GROWTH RATES

The setting of interest rates is one of the tools that governments use to influence economic growth and contain inflation (or the rise in prices). Central banks, many of which are independent government entities, control these key rates as part of their monetary policy. Some central banks have a mandate to keep inflation low (European Central Bank), while other central banks have the dual task of sustaining economic growth *and* containing inflation (U.S. Federal Reserve).

As of the time of this writing, overnight interest rates stand at 0.1 percent in Japan, 0.25 percent in the United

States and Switzerland, 0.50 percent in the United Kingdom, 0.75 percent in Europe, and 1 percent in Canada. Meanwhile, the overnight rates in Oceania are somewhat higher than in other developed countries; they are 2.5 percent in New Zealand and 3.50 percent in Australia. The key lending rates in hot emerging nations are even higher: 6.0 percent in China, 8.0 percent in India, and 8.5 percent in Brazil.

Why do some of these countries have such high interest rates? A high rate of economic growth puts upward pressure on prices (inflation) throughout the economy, and this inflation is not good for individuals who save and invest or for those who are retired and living on a fixed income. By raising interest rates, central banks try to dial down the rate of economic growth somewhat, but particularly they want to bring down the rate of inflation to as low as 2 percent—a pace that is considered benign and manageable.

What happens when global interest rates are all over the place the way they are today? The unintended result of setting overnight rates higher than other nations is that money from abroad (hot money) looking to earn that extra yield flows into the country offering the high rates. As foreign capital comes in, the currency with the high interest rate gains in value. As the local currency appreciates, the country relies more on imports and less on domestic goods. Plus, a strong local currency generally leads to declines in exports and economic growth.

Brazil, Switzerland, and Australia are countries whose currencies are appreciating quite fast. The Brazilian government, upset over the low interest rates in developed countries, is crying foul and is fighting the inflow of foreign capital by raising taxes on hot money.

Other countries, like Switzerland, go even further. The Swiss Central Bank lowered overnight rates close to zero *and* threatened speculators that it would print as much money as necessary to keep the Swiss franc weak relative to the euro. Extreme measures of this kind have been taking place because of the European crisis. For example, as markets have lost confidence in the euro, many people have sold the euro and bought the Swiss franc. (In fact, I was one of these people.) The EURCHF today is arbitrarily trading within a very narrow band above 1.20. The situation is unsustainable and is bound to have an explosive outcome at some point, but it could be months or years before anything happens. For now, and much to my chagrin, trading volume in EURCHF has pretty much dried up.

MARKET INTERCONNECTIONS

As seen in the examples of the arbitrarily low Chinese yuan and Swiss franc rates, the spread of the credit crisis from the United States to Europe, and the impact of U.S. quantitative easing on Brazil, today's global capital and money markets are interconnected. Setting rates for currency markets is one of the ways in which the financial community communicates.

Please keep in mind that seemingly isolated events in distant parts of the world can and do affect the currency rates you will trade. Over time, you will come to understand these subtle correlations and even anticipate their impact on currency markets. I don't recommend that you try to time fundamental movements, because time will pass really slowly. Rather, hold your fundamental views in suspense until the technical analysis justifies placing a trade.

KEY MARKET PERSONALITIES

There are a relatively few big players in currency markets that every forex trader should be acquainted with. By virtue of their elected post or appointment, they have a big podium from which to influence policy that affects currency markets. Table 6-2 gives a quick review of who these people are.

TABLE 6-2 Key Market Personalities

NAME AND TITLE	COUNTRY	NOTES
Barack Obama, president	United States	Although not involved at all on U.S. dollar policy, the U.S. president can commit the United States to policies that could affect the dollar, such as going to war or imposing trade sanctions. Obama is up for reelection in November 2012. Should he win a second term, he will have to contend with major fiscal reform of entitlement programs and tax-rate changes to maintain trust in the long-term viability of U.S. debt.

TABLE 6-2 **Key Market Personalities,** *continued*

NAME AND TITLE	COUNTRY	NOTES
Ben Bernanke, Federal Reserve chairman	United States	When this man sneezes, the United States catches a cold and the globe gets pneumonia, sort of. The U.S. Fed chairman holds immense influence over the perceived value of the U.S. dollar. The chairman's top priority is the U.S. economy, not defending the U.S. dollar. Controversial measures, such as the rescue of AIG, forced mergers of firms, outright purchases of commercial paper, issuance of government guarantees, expansion of the Fed's balance sheet by the US$ trillions, hoarding U.S. securities, and lowering overnight and medium-term rates to near zero, have hurt the dollar. His second four-year term as chairman began in January 2010.
Timothy Geithner, secretary of the Treasury	United States	If Ben Bernanke were Batman, Tim Geithner would be Robin. Also a very important person for the U.S. dollar, the U.S. secretary of the Treasury makes statements like, "It is in the best interest of the United States to keep a strong dollar," whether he means it or not. If there is a verbal or actual joint central bank intervention to calm markets, the U.S. message could be given by either Bernanke or Geithner. Geithner is the face of the United States when criticizing China over its currency policy, but he has always stopped short of branding China a "currency manipulator." He has been in office since January 2009 and may stay for another four years if Obama wins and does not make a Cabinet reshuffle. The market perceives him as an experienced professional.

TABLE 6-2 Key Market Personalities, *continued*

NAME AND TITLE	COUNTRY	NOTES
Angela Merkel, chancellor	Germany	Since the 2005 German elections (and particularly since the onset of the 2010 European crisis), Angela Merkel has wielded influence over the future of Europe (and the euro) like no one else. She is a strong advocate for fiscal discipline. Sensing the winds of political change in France (a key ally of Germany in leading Europe), Merkel is in a quagmire trying to save the eurozone project and standing by governance principles that are often not popular outside of Germany. A worsening of the euro zone crisis will likely hurt more outside of Germany but might be politically costly to Merkel.
Mario Draghi, European Central Bank (ECB) president	European Union	The second most important person for the fate of the euro is Mario Draghi, who is only the third ECB president and started his tenure on November 2011. Italian by birth, he holds considerable credibility and almost universal support from private and public sectors. The gravity of the EU crisis forced him to act in a way closer to Ben Bernanke than to his two orthodox predecessors. Draghi initiated a long-term debt refinancing program (LTRO) that put more than €1.0 trillion in the hands of EU banks to keep them afloat in the face of continued uncertainty over the fate of European policies. Directly and indirectly, he has been providing support for bonds issued by European nations that are under pressure. He should be seen as ready to take whatever measures are needed to support the euro; after all, the fate of the ECB is closely associated with that of the euro.

TABLE 6-2 **Key Market Personalities**, *continued*

NAME AND TITLE	COUNTRY	NOTES
David Cameron, prime minister	United Kingdom	Cameron assumed office May 2010, replacing Gordon Brown. He has had a tense relationship with the European Union, trying to be part of Europe but fighting off EU regulatory changes that would diminish the significant power London has in terms of financial activity. His government also is pushing through robust fiscal reform and banking system overhaul, all things that can and do move GBPUSD and EURGBP.
Sir Mervyn King, Bank of England (BOE) governor	United Kingdom	King took the helm of the Bank of England in July 2003, and his term ends in 2013. He followed the laissez-faire approach of former Fed chairman Alan Greenspan, letting markets grow beyond their boundaries, and was reportedly blindsided when the crisis arrived. He has been a vocal critic of banks since the crisis. Banks are demanding a less critical head of the BOE if they are to stay based in London, and the name of Paul Tucker has surfaced as King's likely successor.
Glenn Stevens, Reserve Bank of Australia (RBA) governor	Australia	Stevens has served as RBA governor since September 2006, and his appointment is up for renewal in 2013. He has been known for being pro-banks and pro-free-market forces. He raised rates 0.50 percent in early 2008, contrary to other central banks, but ultimately dropped them to 3.00 percent. He is important because if continued appreciation of AUDUSD were to become an issue, he'd be the one making that sort of statement.

TABLE 6-2 Key Market Personalities, *continued*

NAME AND TITLE	COUNTRY	NOTES
Masaaki Shirakawa, Bank of Japan (BOJ) governor	Japan	Shirakawa became BOJ governor in April 2008 as the credit crisis began to jump to a new dimension. The BOJ's charter calls for price stability and financial system stability. He has been an advocate of monetary and fiscal discipline to inspire investor confidence. He has been against quantitative easing programs, even after the March 2011 Japan earthquake and tsunami. With him at the helm, the yen and Japanese government bonds (JGBs) have remained strong.
Hu Jintao, president	China	Despite being in the twilight of his second and final five-year term (it ends in 2013), Hu is battling a serious domestic political crisis. His government resisted efforts to speed the yuan's rate of appreciation until April 2012, when the bands of volatility were widened to 1.0 percent from 0.5 percent—a significant step toward bringing the yuan to its true value. His government is also trying to manage a soft landing for the Chinese economy and its continued transition to more financial integration with the West. China is often thought of as a potential savior (source of fresh funds) for European governments and their efforts to gain the market's credibility.
Xi Jinping, vice president	China	The presumptive next president of China as of 2013, he is described by those who know him as "pragmatic, serious, cautious, hardworking, down to earth, and low-key."

SENTIMENT INDICATORS

There are commonplace indicators for gauging the markets' appetite for riskier assets. Just to be clear, the U.S. dollar, the Japanese yen, Treasury securities, and bank deposits are the safest types of investments, and they are what investors hoard when they are afraid. Meanwhile, stocks and various other currencies (the euro, the Australian dollar, and emerging-market currencies) are some of the things investors buy when they feel confident about economic prospects. When the financial world is poised to do well, the United Kingdom's sterling does quite well; London is the center of the global financial world. Also, when the price of crude oil is rising, the Canadian dollar and the Mexican peso also rise; these two are oil-exporting countries. The Australian dollar is also known as a commodity currency, meaning that the export of commodities like livestock is important to it, as is the export of gold.

> **KEY CONCEPT:** Beyond these broad historical correlations,
> there are indicators that are good for getting a sense of who
> controls the mood any given day. If we know which way a
> currency price might "take off" (up, down, or nowhere), we
> can adapt our strategy, take-profit level, and stop-loss level.

I will mention a few indicators that are worth becoming familiar with. Don't feel that you have to track them daily in order to trade, but look at them as a way to get a sense of where the global and the U.S. economy are going and how different important rates are changing over time. Financial websites like Bloomberg.com or Yahoo! Finance carry these charts, if you know how to look for them.

LIBOR-OIS SPREAD

You may never have heard of the LIBOR-OIS spread, and the definition is rather technical, so I will not confuse the novice reader with a lot of details. This rate tells us how afraid banks are to lend money to each other from one day to the next. The normal rate is said to be around 0.20 percent, but as you can tell from Figure 6-1, this rate rose steadily until early January 2012, when it started to decrease. The reason it rose is that the market at large was concerned that Europe was not finding the right solution to deal with its problems. What we can tell from the decline since January is that the market remains jittery compared to last year, but is willing to go along temporarily with the solution that the European Union announced in late December 2011.

THE CBOE VOLATILITY INDEX (VIX INDEX)

The VIX Index is the ticker symbol of an index that tracks how volatile S&P 500 options contracts can get. In simple terms, it is often referred to as the fear index. Let's say a normal value for the VIX is 18. This means that the market expects that after the next 30 days, the S&P 500 will be no more than 5.2 percent up or down. If the VIX reaches 40, then the market

FIGURE 6-1 **LIBOR-OIS Spread**

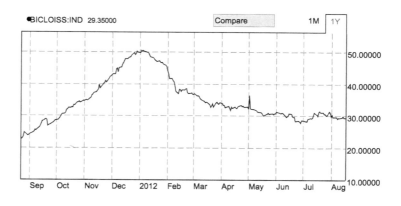

Source: Bloomberg Finance L.P. LOIS3:IND ticker. Used with permission of
Bloomberg Finance L.P.

thinks that the S&P may end the next month no more than
11.5 percent up or down, which is obviously a very big swing.
Figure 6-2 tells us that from August 2011 through the first
half of December 2011, the VIX alarm bells were sounding
loud and clear. Uncertainty was in the air, and the VIX was
one of the main barometers for tracking trader jitters.

THE S&P 500

Just about everyone is familiar with the S&P 500 index, so I
won't go into a lot of detail. It is one of the most recognizable
benchmarks telling us how the cash invested in U.S. stocks
at large is faring. There was an abrupt drop in the value of
the S&P 500 during the August to October period, when the

FIGURE 6-2 **Chicago Board Options Exchange SPX Volatility Index (VIX), Last 12 Months**

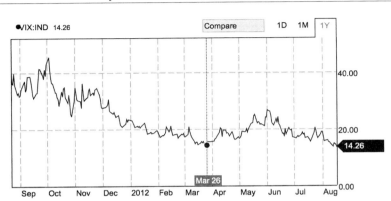

Source: Bloomberg Finance L.P. VIX:IND ticker. Used with permission of Bloomberg Finance L.P.

European crisis was intensifying, but it has since reached a higher level than what it had been at this time last year—a positive sign (see Figure 6-3). Notice that the VIX is almost the mirror image of the S&P 500.

CRUDE OIL PRICES

Crude oil makes the world go round. The two main crude oil benchmark prices are the European Brent crude and the West Texas Sour (WTS) crude, the first generally being higher priced than the second. The importance of crude prices is that they tell us whether demand is rising or falling. It could be rising because there is a perceived shortage of oil or because the global economy needs more oil to sustain

FIGURE 6-3 S&P 500 Index, Last 12 Months

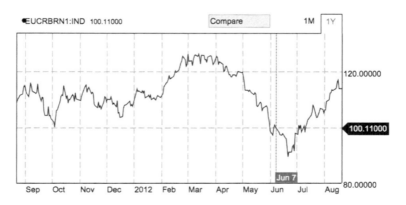

Source: Bloomberg Finance L.P. SPX:IND ticker. Used with permission of Bloomberg
Finance L.P. Reproduced with permission of S&P Dow Jones Indices LLC.

FIGURE 6-4 European Brent Crude Oil Spot, Last 12 Months

Source: Bloomberg Finance L.P. EUCRBRN1:IND ticker. Used with permission of
Bloomberg Finance L.P.

growth. Over the past year, crude prices have been more than
US$100/barrel, a threshold that is rather high for economies
to recover quickly. In Figure 6-4, see how Brent crude prices
rose as the European situation improved in February 2012.

FIGURE 6-5 U.S. Generic 10-Year Bond Yield, Last 12 Months

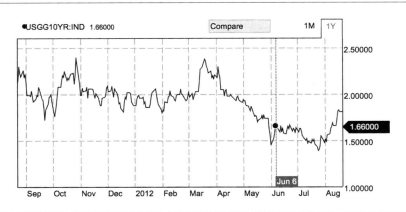

Source: Bloomberg Finance L.P. USGG10YR:IND ticker. Used with permission of Bloomberg Finance L.P.

THE 10-YEAR U.S. BOND YIELD

The chart of the 10-year U.S. bond yield (Figure 6-5) reveals what levels of long-term interest rates are ahead for the United States based on what we know now. If we expect rates to be 2.0 percent 10 years from now, then in theory we should be willing to borrow at today's rate, lend it to a business for 10 years at 5 percent, and keep the difference. That's the general idea behind the actions of the Fed's Bernanke: to force banks to put their capital to productive use by lending it and escaping the low interest rates offered by short- and long-term U.S. Treasury bills, notes, and bonds. Is it working? It's too early to tell. If the 10-year bond yield keeps falling, it will be a clear sign that his plan is not working.

Your First Trading Strategy

Every day, we drive a certain distance in going to work and earning an income. In the process, we become familiar with the road and the landmarks, shops, and billboards between our home and our work. We know how long it should take us to complete the trip based on the time of day when we travel. When traffic conditions become difficult, we typically know whether we should use a different road. We know this because the road becomes very familiar to us.

As I mentioned in the first chapter, forex traders seek specific profit targets each day—for example, an average profit of 20 pips per day. More often than not, a trader becomes very familiar with his trading strategy and with the behavior of his favorite currency pair at different times of the day and throughout the week. He develops an intuition for the optimal time to get into and out of a trade.

This chapter is absolutely critical because it gives the reader a road map for becoming a focused forex driver. We will cover how to set performance targets. You will learn a simple yet effective forex trading strategy.

For the driving analogy I use in this book, the trading strategy is your *destination*. More than 90 percent of the destinations to or from which you drive are relatively constant: work or school, the store, church, friends' homes, the mall, the gym, and so on. Perhaps you use 10 percent of your time in the car to drive to new, exotic, and fun destinations. I should mention that there are some more exotic and challenging trading strategies (with greater potential risk/reward) that you may want to explore further as you become a more proficient trader. For now, let's keep it simple and fully comprehend a proven strategy, the VT Pivot Roadmap.

The VT Pivot Roadmap Strategy

The VT Pivot Roadmap is a high-probability trading strategy. It might be the first of many strategies that you learn. Then again, some of you might like it so much that it will be the only trading strategy you will use.

On the web, traders can find several trading strategies based on pivot lines. I created this particular pivot strategy for VaraTrade (www.varatrade.com), a portal dedicated to bringing together reputable trader education materials. The VT Pivot Roadmap strategy is the *unique combination* of pivot lines and rules that I have developed through more than 10 years of forex market experience.

Many retail traders look at pivot lines as just one more technical indicator. But institutional forex traders, who control the majority of forex trading volume, have a sound appreciation for pivot lines and for the companion pivot support/resistance lines.

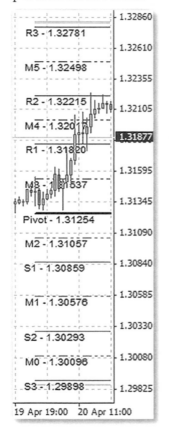

The chart to the left shows the pivot line as a heavy line, and also shows six support and six resistance lines. The pivot support and resistance lines have peculiar names that are important for you to memorize.

Pivot support lines. The support line closest to the pivot is called S1, the next is called S2, and the lowest is called S3.

Pivot resistance lines. The resistance line closest to the pivot is called R1, the next is called R2, and the highest is called R3.

Pivot midpoint lines. There are six midpoint lines: three above the pivot line and three below the pivot line.

Midpoint support lines. The first midpoint support line is M0, and it is located between S3 and S2; the next, M1, is between S2 and S1; and M2 is found between S1 and the pivot line. M2 is very important because of a rule we will discuss shortly.

Midpoint resistance lines. The first midpoint resistance line above the pivot is M3, and it is located between the pivot line and R1; next comes M4, located between R1 and R2. Finally, M5 is located between R2 and R3. M3 is very important because of another rule we discuss shortly.

> **KEY CONCEPT:** The technical descriptions of pivot lines given here apply to all currency pairs and tradable securities, but the rules of engagement that I describe next apply primarily to the EURUSD pair, the most liquid of all.

THE PIVOT-LINE CHALLENGE

Pivot lines have something of a magnetic pull on currency prices. I also like to compare pivot lines to the *muleta* (or small red cape) used by bullfighters to challenge the bull—with the currency price being the bull in this analogy. Just as most bulls will charge the *muleta*, so there is a *challenge of the pivot line* most days. This means that the EURUSD will almost always make an attempt to cross the pivot line. Armed with this insight, you can use the euro's repetitive behavior to create a profitable trading opportunity.

This so-called challenge of the pivot line may come as early as GMT 00:00 (the start of the Asian session), or as late as 23:00 GMT. Some traders look at the New York close as the start of the new trading day, but this stategy is based on the start of a new day a few hours later—at GMT 00:00 to be precise. Depending on where you are in the world, you could trade this strategy during your evenings if you are in the United States, or during your mornings to early evening if you are in the Asia-Pacific region.

Compared to the European and American sessions, the Asian session is a slow-moving period for EURUSD. So it might be surprising to experienced traders to know that there are excellent chances to capture a net 20 to 40 pips during a quiet period of the day. The majority of EURUSD traders prefer to trade this pair during the European session until 11 a.m. New York time. Important economic announcements from Europe and the United States make this a very volatile period for currency markets. However, a volatile environment is not necessarily the best place for beginners to try to learn forex. Economic announcements from Tokyo and Australia generally have little impact on EURUSD prices, so what ultimately leads the euro to move in recurrent patterns remains a mystery to me. We are not going to try to decipher exactly what is the cause of these movements; instead, we will try to spot high-probability trade setups.

The March 12 to March 21, 2012, period depicted in Figure 7-1 is rather typical of trading conditions. I wanted to pick a consecutive 10-day period (eight trading sessions) to show you how the VT Pivot Roadmap strategy can be adapted to various market conditions. We will go into detail later in this chapter. For now, notice that EURUSD did not cross the pivot line every day. But, as the arrows show, the euro made an effort to reach the pivot line (the pivot challenge) every one of those days. The space seen between the

FIGURE 7-1 VT Pivot Roadmap, EURUSD 1-Hour Chart

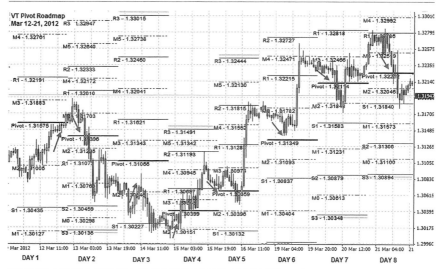

Note: Each candle represents a 1-hour period.

support and resistance lines from day to day varies based on the amount of price change on the previous day—some days have wilder fluctuations than others.

THE VT PIVOT LINE INDICATOR

At one second past midnight (GMT), the pivot line for the next 24 hours can be calculated and drawn on a platform chart. There are at least four different versions of pivot lines available on the web (floor pivot, Woodie's, Camarilla, and DeMark's). My pivot calculations are in line with the floor pivot point calculation, which is the most popular version of the four. I found calculating and drawing the pivot lines each day very cumbersome, so I developed what is called a *custom indicator* that automatically draws the 13 pivot lines for the EURUSD on my MT4 trading platform each day. I wanted this indicator to be much more than a pivot-line indicator, though. I conducted statistical analyses of the volatility of the EURUSD at different times of the day. My goal was to visualize how far up or down the euro could move on a normal day and during extreme market conditions.

The indicator in Figure 7-2 displays various components. The upper band of volatility (upper shaded section) shows how high the euro could go at a specific time of day. The lower band of volatility (lower shaded section) shows how low the euro has been known to fall at a specific time of day. The white space between the upper and lower bands of volatility is the section of normal volatility. Notice that the size of the bands of volatility and normal volatility vary depending on the time of day. Each hour the indicator generates the upper and lower shaded bands for the upcoming 60 minutes, leaving a blank space (the box on the upper right margin of Figure 7-2). Seeing the range in which the euro is likely to trade over the next hour is a big leg up if you are monitoring an open trade or a potential trade entry.

This indicator is available at www.VaraTrade.com/pivot lines.htm under the name VT Pivot Lines. E-mail info@ varatrade.com and mention your book purchase to get a six-month free trial of the indicator.

FIGURE 7-2 VT Pivot Roadmap Indicator, EURUSD 15-Minute Chart

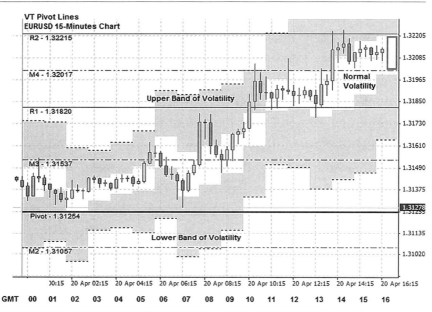

Note: Each candle represents a 15-minute period.

VT PIVOT ROADMAP PROBABILITIES

If we flipped a coin repeatedly (say a thousand times) to decide whether to buy or sell anything, we would come very close to 50 percent buy decisions and 50 percent sell decisions. Each coin flip is unique and has the same chances of being heads or tails. The VT Pivot Roadmap strategy, like any trading strategy worth trying, relies on considerably better probabilities than coin flipping—or monkey dart throwing, for that matter.

FIGURE 7-3 Odds that the EURUSD Will Cross the Pivot Line Any Given Day

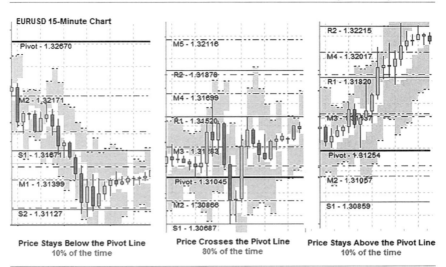

Price Stays Below the Pivot Line
10% of the time

Price Crosses the Pivot Line
80% of the time

Price Stays Above the Pivot Line
10% of the time

Note: Each candle represents a 1-hour period.

Based on a price study I conducted with seven years' worth of daily prices (2003–2010), I found the following (see Figure 7-3):

- The average pip distance between EURUSD at 00:01 GMT and the new pivot line is 21 pips—this number is significant because we would like to target at least 20 pips per day.
- The odds that EURUSD will *move toward and cross* the pivot line at some point during the day are 80 percent.
- The odds that the day's *low* price for EURUSD will be *higher* than the pivot line are only 10 percent.

- The odds of the *high* price of the EURUSD being *lower* than the pivot line are also 10 percent.

There is one more set of probabilities to keep in mind. If the price of EURUSD crosses the pivot line, the *high* price will be at least 20 pips higher than the pivot line 82 percent of the time.

At GMT 00:01, we don't know what the EURUSD daily high for the coming 24 hours will be, but we do know this:

- The pivot-line value and whether the pivot line was crossed or not.
- The EURUSD *high* price will be *above* the pivot line 90 percent of the time (80 percent probability that the pivot line is crossed plus 10 percent probability that the price will stay above the pivot line).
- We can even estimate that 66 percent of the time, the EURUSD daily high will be more than 20 pips above the pivot line (80 percent probability of a pivot-line cross times 82 percent probability that the daily high will be 20 or more pips higher than the pivot line; see Figure 7-4).

What does all this set of mumbo jumbo probabilities mean to you?

It means a lot if EURUSD starts the day (GMT 00:00) *below* the pivot line. You have a 90 percent chance that the daily high will be above the pivot line. So if at the start of the day you see a EURUSD price that is set to rise from where it

FIGURE 7-4 Probabilities of Daily High if Pivot Line Is Crossed, EURUSD

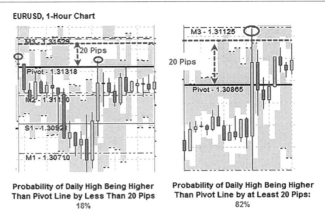

Probability of Daily High Being Higher Than Pivot Line by Less Than 20 Pips
18%

Probability of Daily High Being Higher Than Pivot Line by at Least 20 Pips:
82%

Note: Each candle represents a 1-hour period.

now is to at least the pivot line, what should you be inclined to do? Hint: have you heard of "buy low, sell high"? You would want to *buy* EURUSD.

It also means that if you are starting a *buy* EURUSD below the pivot line, a potential profit target could be set 20 pips above the pivot line—you would have an 82 percent chance of reaching that target *if* the pivot line is crossed. A word of caution: before you spring to buy EURUSD anytime it starts the day below the pivot line, read the next section.

VT PIVOT ROADMAP STRATEGY RULES

The goal of all aspects of our trading is to make it as mechanical and rules-based as possible. The VT Pivot Roadmap strategy has some guiding principles:

- If EURUSD at GMT 00:01 is below the pivot line *and* if it reaches the targeted entry-level point, I would *buy* the euro.
- If EURUSD at GMT 00:01 is above the pivot line *and* if it reaches the targeted entry-level point, I would *sell* the euro.

Bear in mind that the best time to buy or sell is not always right at 00:01 or even in the first (GMT) hour of the day. When it comes to entering into a trade, here are some basic rules for trading the VT Pivot Roadmap strategy successfully:

Rule 1. The targeted entry point at which to *buy* EURUSD is an area between 40 and 50 pips *below* the pivot line. Using the pivot support lines as references, the ideal area is within 5 pips of the second midpoint support line (M2) and 5 pips away from the first pivot support line (S1).

Rule 2. The targeted entry point at which to *sell* EURUSD is an area that is between 40 and 50 pips *above* the pivot line. The ideal is an area that is within 5 pips of the third midpoint support line (M3) and 5 pips away from the first resistance line (R1).

Rule 3. It is *not* wise to trade using the pivot roadmap strategy at times when:

- The day's open (GMT 00:01) is within 15 pips of the pivot line.
- We believe the pivot challenge has taken place.
- Something dramatic is causing the euro to rally or sink more than usual.

The common element for Rules 1 and 2 is that they both require a trader to exercise patience. I cannot emphasize this enough. Having the patience to achieve the right entry point will ultimately determine whether you earn or lose money trading.

KEY CONCEPT: Right after the day's open at 00:01 GMT, the EURUSD price will typically "dance around," meaning that prices will hover close to the day's open level plus or minus 10 to 15 pips. Although this is not infallible, the EURUSD does not usually challenge the pivot line directly. It first acquires enough **momentum** by going in the opposite direction and then taking a hard swing toward the pivot line.

To illustrate this point of momentum, I will use an analogy of a *professional* wrestling technique. Have you seen a match in which one of the wrestlers strikes the opponent in the center of the ring, then runs into the ring ropes to gain speed and try to hit the opponent even harder? If you haven't, this analogy might not make sense. But if you have seen this move, then you should keep it in mind because that is what the EURUSD typically does after the day's open.

Setting Adequate Targets and Protection

Buying the EURUSD if the price is below the pivot line at the start of the day may be attractive based on what we've talked about. But we are now going to cover why it's best to wait for the right conditions to buy the euro. The reason for this abundance of caution is that I want you to learn to limit yourself to a 1 to 2 percent trade risk setup. In other words, if you buy EURUSD right at the daily open and don't use a stop-loss level, you may expose the account to a loss of more than 2 percent.

> **KEY CONCEPT:** Currency prices do not usually move in a straight line. Most of the time, they move in a weaving pattern: up, down, up, down. Before you achieve the 20 or 30 pips you are aiming for, currency prices may move in the opposite direction from your trade objective.

To put it simply, if you buy EURUSD before the euro takes its normal downward movement, your stop loss of 20 or 30 pips may be triggered, which would cause you to have a losing trade. I would never buy the euro right at the open unless the open point is 50 to 60 pips away from the pivot line. One of the first steps I take each day is to measure the distance in pips between M2 and the pivot line. If it is 30 pips or less, I definitely wait for the euro to drop below M2 by 10 to 15 pips before I look for the challenge to the pivot line. If it does not fall to this level, I will not buy EURUSD that day. I need a solid 40 pips between M2 and the pivot line to

FIGURE 7-5 Buying the EURUSD—Setting an Adequate Target and Protection

Note: Each candle represents a 1-hour period.

consider using M2 as the place from which to buy the euro. Another step I take daily is to look at the previous day's low. If the new day's open is within 20 to 30 pips of the previous day's low, I expect the euro to establish a new daily low that is at least a few pips lower than the previous day's low.

As an example, let's say that you are thinking of putting on a *buy* EURUSD order at one of three places: (1) at the daily open, (2) at the M2 line, or (3) at about the previous day's low (Figure 7-5). Whatever entry point you choose, you have decided to use a 30-pip stop loss and have a 40-pip profit target.

Table 7-1 illustrates a few important things:

- It matters a lot whether we enter into a trade.
- A reasonable profit can be made even when the pivot line is not crossed.

TABLE 7-1 Comparing Alternatives to Select an Entry Point

	STARTING PRICE	STOP-LOSS PRICE	TARGET PRICE	PROFIT (LOSS)
Buy at open	1.3078	1.3048 (triggered)	1.3118 (not triggered)	−30 pips
Buy at M2 line	1.3064	1.3034 (triggered)	1.3104 (not triggered)	−30 pips
Buy at previous day's low	1.3045	1.3015 (not triggered)	1.3085 (triggered)	+40 pips

Results derived from Figure 7-5

It is worth noting that if someone in our example had entered a trade at the day's open (1.3078) and had not set a stop loss, she would be looking at a potential loss of 65 to 70 pips that might continue to grow if the trade were not closed. It is best to close trades that go contrary to our predictions early enough, and 30 pips is usually a good amount of pips to risk. If you feel that you need to have a wider stop loss, then you should decrease your trade size accordingly.

SETTING THE APPROPRIATE TRADE SIZE

In my view, this small section is one of the most important in the whole book. We've gone over examples that show bad results for those who, perhaps without noticing, make a trade that is bigger than it should be. At the back of the book (Appendix B), you can find an easy reference table that tells you how much you should risk based on the account size and the account type (mini or standard).

Let's say that you reside in the United States (50:1 leverage) and you start a mini demo account of US$5,000; the appendix table would tell you that you could place a trade of up to 1.7 mini lots. This table is conservative by forex trading standards, as the suggested trade size limits the risk to a trading account to 1.0 percent, assuming a 30-pip stop loss. When your balance increases to, say, US$6,000, then you could trade using 2.0 mini lots.

Personally, I usually place trades that are worth 50 percent of this "normal" amount, but if I feel really good about a trade setup, I will trade the full normal recommended size. In exceptional occasions, I will venture as much as 2.0 percent in a trade—always with an appropriate stop loss in place.

Bear in mind that if you are fond of trading pairs that carry a high pip value (EURGBP, USDJPY, EURJPY, GBPJPY), you should ensure that your trade size is about 20 percent smaller than what is recommended in Appendix B. But just to clarify further, do not use the VT Pivot Roadmap strategy with a currency pair other than EURUSD.

If you wish to see a trade-size table that is shown in Appendix B for different currencies or leverage levels, you can request a copy at info@varatrade.com, subject line "trade size."

PLACING A LIMIT ORDER

Before we examine the pivot strategy in action during a 10-day period, I will show you how easy it is to set a limit

FIGURE 7-6 Setting Up a Limit Order

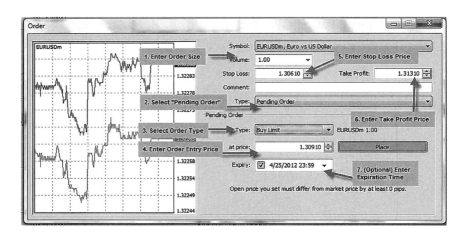

order. You follow the same steps as for placing a regular market order—double-click on the desired currency pair. Once the order pop-up appears, you follow the steps shown in Figure 7-6.

There are four types of pending orders that you should learn by heart: buy limit, buy stop, sell limit, and sell stop (Figure 7-7). Buy stop and sell stop orders are orders to take advantage of breakouts (when the price departs abruptly up or down from a known formation). One way to tell these four orders apart is to remind yourself to "stop" placing breakout orders until you are ready to use them; thus, you would use only buy limit and sell limit orders and not buy stop and sell stop orders.

In Figure 7-7, we see that EURUSD is falling toward 1.3300. We are contemplating a few scenarios:

FIGURE 7-7 **Types of Pending Orders**

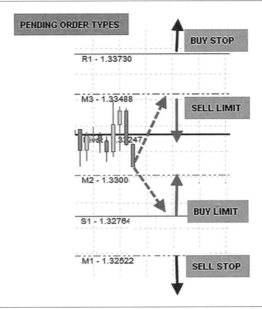

- If the EURUSD falls to the S1 line and then rebounds, we could place a *buy limit* order at 1.32764.
- If the EURUSD rebounds to M3 and we expect it to fall from there, we could place a *sell limit* order at 1.33488.
- Let's say you see a serious chance that the EURUSD will do really badly and break a major support level at 1.3260 after a major economic announcement. In this case, you could place a *sell stop* at 1.32522.
- Let's say you also believe that the euro could rally with the stock market past a key resistance level at 1.3365. You could place a *buy stop* order at 1.3373.

PUTTING THIS STRATEGY INTO PRACTICE— EIGHT TRADING DAYS

To further solidify how to start applying the VT Pivot Roadmap strategy, I will take a closer look at the large graph in Figure 7-1 and apply the principles you learned one day at a time. Any potential profits and losses in this exercise are hypothetical for the March 12 to March 21, 2012, period for which we provide the actual prices. Each candle in the chart below represents one hour, with light-shaded bullish candles and dark-shaded bearish candles.

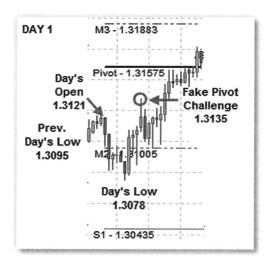

On *Day 1* of our eight-trading day exercise (at GMT 00:01, to be precise), we can verify that the day's open was EURUSD 1.3121 and that the pivot line is 1.3158 (rounded up from 1.31575). Rule 1 applies and tentatively tells us to buy the EURUSD. Next, we proceed to the checks of Rule 3. We check for minimum distance between the daily open and the pivot line and verify that the distance between these two points on Day 1 is 37 pips. We pass this check and now read the news and check the economic calendar to verify that indeed nothing out of the normal is happening with the euro. We now have the green light to look for an ideal trade entry point.

Looking at a previous day's low of 1.3095 and an M2 line of 1.3100, we set a buy limit of EURSD 1.3091, with a stop loss that is 30 pips below (1.3061) and a profit target of 40 pips (1.3131).

As we see in the chart, for the first five hour candles the euro is moving away from the pivot line and toward our trade-entry level. The day's low (1.3078) is established at GMT 05:00, but it does not touch our stop loss of 1.3061. Remember the wrestler analogy. When the euro hits a low point, it often uses that momentum to go in the opposite direction. By GMT 10:00, there is a fake pivot challenge that hits 1.3135 and takes us out of our trade at 1.3131 for a 38-pip profit (40 pips minus the spread of 2 pips).

So, that's a nice outcome for Day 1, but a natural question is: do I have to stay up through the night and monitor this trade? The answer is no. You can leave a limit order in place with the specifications that we developed for the entry price, the stop loss, and the take profit. After you have set the pending order details on the trading platform, you can go to bed or to work.

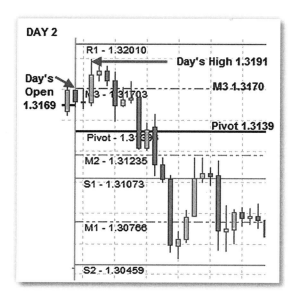

Day 2 starts with EURUSD at 1.3169, very near the daily high of the previous day (1.3172) and the 1.3170 M3 line. Rule 2 tells us to tentatively place a *sell* EURSD trade. As we check for Rule 3, we note that the pivot line is 30 pips away from the open and passes our first check. We also check the mood on the euro and find that Rule 3 is fully satisfied. As we proceed to determine a good entry point, we think that the distance from the M3 line to the pivot line at 1.3139 is tight—a mere 30 pips away—and decide to place a *sell limit* EURUSD order at 1.3179, with a stop loss at 1.3209 and a profit target of 1.3139, which is the pivot line.

After setting our sell limit order, we let the market give us a profit or a loss. Ten hours later, the order is filled and produces our second 38-pip profit. So far so good; we're well on our way to having a 100-pip week.

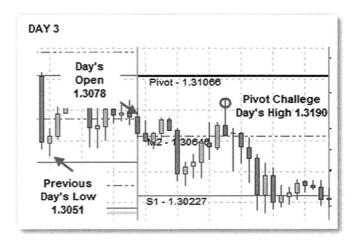

Day 3 may look familiar because we talked about it earlier (in Figure 7-5 and Table 7-1). We start the day at 1.3078, and we have about 29 pips distance to the pivot line. Rule 1 and Rule 3 tell us that it is OK to place a buy limit order. Looking at the previous day's low (1.3051) and thinking that the euro will fall before it makes a pivot challenge, we decide to place a *buy limit* order at 1.3045, with a 1.3015 stop loss and a 1.3085 profit target.

As we saw earlier, it is possible to carve out a 40-pip profit during days when the EURUSD does not cross the pivot line. Our limit order is filled at GMT 05:00, our stop loss holds intact, and the daily challenge at GMT 11:00 brings us to our profit target. The stars appear to have aligned in our favor, and we capture another 38 pips, but I have learned to expect this kind of streak to be interrupted by trading losses. Losses, too, sometimes come by twos or threes.

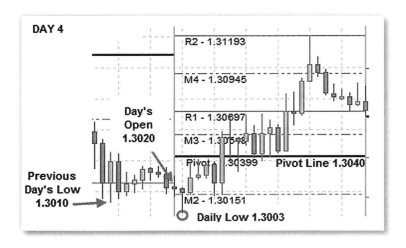

The euro begins *Day 4* at 1.3020, near the previous day's low of 1.3010. The pivot line is 20 pips away from the open at 1.3040. Again, Rule 1 and Rule 3 give us the green light to place a buy limit order. We'd like to do so from 40 or more pips below the pivot line. Something you should know is that price behavior near a "big figure" like 1.3000 or 1.3500 is quite interesting. The natural pattern is for big figures to act like barriers. So if we hope to get into our trade at 1.3000, we are going to have a tough time of it. But let's say that we stick to our policy of starting trades that are at least 40 pips away from the pivot line. We place a *buy limit* order at 1.3000, with a 1.2970 stop loss and a 1.3040 profit target. As we see on the chart above, the day's low was 1.3003 and our pending order was not triggered, meaning that we neither made nor lost money.

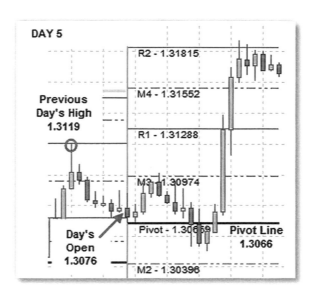

Day 5, a Friday (Thursday night in the United States), starts at 1.3076, a mere 10 pips away from the pivot line. Rule 2 would say that we should place a *sell* EURUSD trade, but Rule 3 overrides it and tells us not to trade using the VT Pivot Roadmap strategy. It is as simple as that.

One of the reasons why I have adopted Rule 3 is that I interpret days of this kind (daily open less than 15 pips away from the pivot line) as days of indecision. Once the pivot line has been crossed, the behavior of prices does not follow the patterns and probabilities that I discuss in the book.

KEY CONCEPT: It is *as important* to know when *not* to trade as to know when we *should* trade.

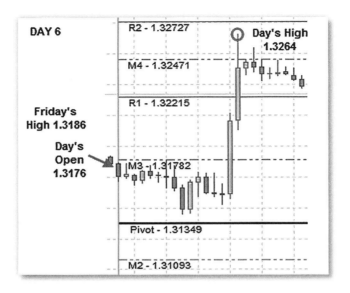

For *Day 6*, the day's open (1.3176) is 41 pips away from the pivot line. Rule 2 tells us to place a sell limit trade, and Rule 3 gives us the green light to do so. We are also looking at Friday's high of 1.3186 and believe it would be good to set an entry point above M3 (1.3178). Let's assume that by the time we calculate things, EURUSD has dropped 10 pips and it is no longer attractive to place the trade. We decide to set a resting *sell limit* order at EURUSD 1.3182, with a stop loss at 1.3212 and a profit target of 1.3142. As it turns out, this is one of those 1-out-of-5 days when the pivot line is not crossed. The euro establishes a low of 1.3141, but our resting order was not triggered until after the pivot challenge took place. Let's say we were asleep when the pivot challenge happened and we could not cancel the resting order. The net result is that the order is activated at GMT 15:00 and our stop loss is hit an hour later for a 30-pip loss.

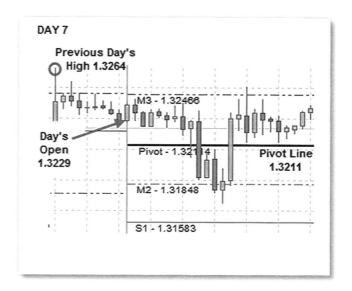

For *Day 7*, the open price (1.3229) is a mere 18 pips above the pivot line. Rule 2 tells us to place a sell limit order. Keeping Rule 3 in mind, this is a borderline case. In order for this trade to be worthwhile, two things must happen: the euro has to rise to about the previous day's high *and* the pivot challenge must not have taken place by the time we are put into the trade.

This is one of those trades that needs "babysitting," meaning that I would not set a limit order and go to bed. If I intend to be up and watch it, I would place a limit order. If I wasn't able to watch it, I would not place the trade. Let's say I stay up and set a pending order; it would be a *sell limit* order with an entry of 1.3264 (the previous day's high), a stop loss of 1.3294, and a take profit of 1.3224. I wait a few hours, checking regularly to see if this trade was activated. At GMT 09:00, the EURUSD crosses the pivot line without having activated my trade. I cancel the pending order. No gain—more important, no loss.

On *Day 8*, the EURUSD starts the day at 1.3237, 12 pips above the pivot line. Rule 2 tells me to place a sell limit order, but the trade idea does not pass the minimum distance of Rule 3. I stay out of this trading opportunity. As you become more experienced and develop your own set of trading rules (part of what I call a forex trading plan), you will determine whether it's worth taking a risk on a trade like this. I can see how someone could take this trade because (1) EURUSD has risen to R1 without challenging the pivot line, and (2) there is a substantial 54 pips to the pivot line. I think if someone were to take this trade, he should cut the size of it in half (compared to whatever size he usually trades) and set a stop loss of 20 pips instead of 30 pips. In hindsight, it would have been a profitable trade, but at the time we know only that the odds are mixed but are still attractive.

> **KEY CONCEPT:** As much as I like to earn 100 net pips per week, it is more important to me to keep my risk low, take good trading opportunities when they come, and hold losses to a minimum. This book opens your eyes to new trading opportunities. A major mistake would be to think that these trading techniques will make a great trading opportunity available every day—wouldn't that be nice? The only ways that I know of to help us to find more trading opportunities in a given day are to (1) learn new techniques from top traders or educators and (2) develop your own trading strategies over time.

Following Your Trading Plan

Two of my three teenage daughters are at that scary age when they are learning how to drive. My top concern as I help them practice their driving is their safety. To a lesser extent, I also have the safety of the vehicle and of other drivers in mind.

When a new driver lacks discipline, he can take fatal and/or expensive risks. The rules I am teaching my daughters—like holding the wheel with both hands—are meant to imprint on their nonconscious mind certain habits that will keep them safe.

In essence, my rules stress things that my daughters have learned in driver's education class but also go beyond the things they learned there. In that same spirit, the rules that I share with you in this chapter are what I would do if I were starting over as a trader and knew the things that I know now.

A collection of rules and goals is what forms a trading plan. The trading plan explained in this chapter is meant to be a thorough frame of reference to guide you in your trading. If you trade using a different trading strategy from the one in this book, you could use the format and sample rules given here as a pattern for your own trading plan. Your trading plan *has* to be tailored to the trading strategy that you intend to use. This customized trading plan that I will have you work on will incorporate your various preferences and goals.

Most of us have problems with a critical skill that we need to have if we are to become successful traders. That essential skill—discipline—can be defined as training that is expected to produce a specific character or pattern of behavior.

The thing about discipline is that it is really acquired one day at a time. Until this forex trading plan becomes second nature, I strongly advise you to look for trading opportunities daily and to take the five minutes necessary to read the trading plan *every time you trade*. I recommend that you print it and keep the printout of your plan by your trading computer.

In the plan, you will find boldfaced words and numbers that you may want to change and make them your own. A Word (digital) version of the trading plan is available to registered users of VaraTrade.com upon request—send an e-mail to info@varatrade.com with the subject line "trading plan."

Sample Trading Plan

TRADING GOALS

- Within a **three-month** period ending **April 2013,** I will have my first **100 pips** per week, net of trading losses and trading costs.
- I will limit my trading losses to no more than **3 percent (ever),** but usually to no more than **1 percent,** and I will keep within these limits by using the trade sizes recommended in Appendix B.
- After **one full month** of earning more than **80 net pips per week** on a demo account, I will start trading with a **$1,000** live trading account.
- After **one full month** of earning **100 net pips per week** on a **$1,000** live account, I will fund my trading account with an additional **$4,000.**
- I will stick to the trading strategy of this plan for the next **six months** not adding to the complexity of my trading experience until I am able to achieve these goals.
- I will continue to reinvest my profits until my account reaches a balance of **$75,000,** at which point I will withdraw **100 percent** of my original capital **($5,000).**
- Once I have removed my initial capital, I will withdraw **50 percent** of my monthly earnings and let the rest continue to be reinvested in the trading account.

TRADING DISCIPLINE

- I commit to either trading with discipline or not trading at all.
- I will conduct my currency trading in two practice accounts: one account (demo 1) in which I will follow the trading strategy and

this trading plan strictly, and one account (demo 2) in which I will be free to experiment with different strategies and currencies. If and when I run out of practice money in my demo 2 account, I will start a new demo 2 account.

- I will treat my demo 1 trading account as if it were the life savings of a dear family member, and I will not make foolish bets with it.
- Trading in a live account will follow the rules of this trading plan 100 percent of the time.
- I will read this trading plan and visualize the habits of a disciplined, consistently profitable trader on a daily basis.

CURRENCY TRADED

- EURUSD will be the only currency that I will trade for the foreseeable future. At some point, I might add some currency pairs that are not correlated with EURUSD, such as USDJPY, AUDJPY, or GBPCAD. I understand that I need to have a proven trading strategy for any additional currency pair that I wish to trade.
- Should I start trading a new currency pair, I will go back to using two demo accounts for this currency pair until I validate my trading strategy once more.

TRADING SCHEDULE

- I will trade **four to five days per week.** I will adjust my trading hours to fit the VT Pivot Roadmap strategy: starting on **Sunday night** and going through **Thursday evening,** from **GMT 00:00** to no later than **GMT 06:00.**

(16

TRADE SIZE AND RISK MANAGEMENT

- I will follow the suggested trade sizes in Appendix B, but I may decrease the suggested trade size if the potential risk/return is higher than normal or if my confidence in the trade entry point is lower than desired.
- I will always trade with a stop loss set at the start of the trade. I will not increase or remove my stop loss to stay on a trade.
- I will not leave trades unattended or open overnight without a stop loss, and I will *never* leave trades open over the weekend.

TRADING STRATEGY

- I will use the VT Pivot Roadmap strategy for EURUSD. This is a proven strategy that predicts the EURUSD price behavior relative to the daily pivot line. The VT Pivot Roadmap strategy identifies high-probability trade setups from GMT 00:00 with average profit targets of 40 pips while risking no more than 30 pips.
- **TRADE'S DIRECTION.** The strategy's principles indicate whether to buy or sell EURUSD, such that
  - □ If EURUSD at GMT 00:01 is below the pivot line and reaches the targeted entry-level point, I will set an entry point to *buy* the euro.
  - □ If EURUSD at GMT 00:01 is above the pivot line and reaches the targeted entry-level point, I will set an entry point to *sell* the euro.
- **IDEAL TRADE ENTRY.** The strategy has three clear rules to estimate an ideal trade entry:
  - □ *Rule 1.* The targeted entry point at which to *buy* EURUSD is an area between 40 and 50 pips *below* the pivot line. Using

the pivot support lines as references, the ideal *buy* entry area is typically within 5 pips of the second midpoint support line (M2) and 5 pips away from the first pivot support line (S1). A useful point of reference might be the previous day's low. If the previous day's low is located between M2 and S1, an attractive *buy* entry point is the previous day's close.

□ *Rule 2.* The targeted entry point at which to *sell* EURUSD is an area between 40 and 50 pips *above* the pivot line. The ideal area is within 5 pips of the third midpoint support line (M3) and 5 pips away from the first resistance line (R1). A useful point of reference might be the previous day's high. If the previous day's high is located between M3 and R1, an attractive *sell* entry point is 5 to 10 pips below the previous day's high.

The third rule of the VT Pivot Roadmap strategy indicates when *not* to trade using the strategy:

□ *Rule 3.* It is *not* wise to trade using the Pivot Roadmap strategy at times when:

- The day's open (GMT 00:01) is within 15 pips of the pivot line.
- I believe the pivot challenge has taken place before the EURUSD reaches my targeted entry price,
- Something dramatic is causing the euro to rally or sink more than usual.

PRETRADE ROUTINE

- I will perform pretrade reconnaissance between **GMT 23:45** and **GMT 00:15,** during which time I will systematically evaluate whether to take a trade and, if so, at what levels.

- **NOTES.** I will read the notes I wrote in my trade journal yesterday.
- **MOOD.** I will look for sharp EURUSD movement during the last 24 hours (Rule 3), particularly:
  - If the day closed near the *low* or the high
  - If the EURUSD rose or dropped more than 120 pips from the previous day's open
  - If there was no clear pivot-line challenge

  If I see this kind of sharp price movement and determine that the euro is in a very bullish or very bearish mood, I will not use the trading strategy. I will then note that in my trade journal and start the process of trade evaluation tomorrow.
- **MOOD (2).** To better gauge the mood prevailing in the EURUSD market, I will take a few minutes to look at the important economic announcements that were released the previous day and those that will be released within the next 24 hours to determine whether:
  - Any past economic release came in well above or below expectations.
  - Any important EU or U.S. personality said anything that caused a change in market expectations or made market fears worsen.
  - The market is trading quietly because it is awaiting a major announcement.

  If I determine that the mood in EURUSD is relatively normal, I will continue my trade preparation.
- **MINIMUM DISTANCE.** I will evaluate whether the distance in pips between the EURUSD open price (GMT 00:00) and the new pivot line is at least 15 pips. If it is not, then I will not use the strategy

today. If it is close to 15 pips and I decide to trade, I will do so using a smaller trade size. If the distance is greater than 20 pips, I will continue with preparation for a potential trade opportunity.

- **TRADE DIRECTION.** I will evaluate the appropriate trade direction. If Rule 1 applies, I will set an ideal entry price to buy EURUSD; if Rule 2 applies, I will set an ideal entry price to sell EURUSD.

- **PRICE BARRIERS.** I will look for natural price barriers that may interfere with EURUSD reaching my ideal trade entry level or my targeted profit level. These barriers include:

  - *Long-dated (important) trend lines.* I will draw a soft gray horizontal line to identify the two or three closest important trend lines.

  - *Closest big figures* (EURUSD 1.3000, 1.3500, and 1.4000 especially, but also 1.3100, 1.3200, and so on). I will draw a light green horizontal line to identify the closest or two closest big figures.

  - *Important Fibonacci levels.* I will draw a Fibonacci retracement on my 4-hour EURUSD chart.

  - *Important moving averages.* I will look at the 40- and 80-period simple moving averages (SMA) on my 4-hour EURUSD chart.

  - *Previous day's low and high.* I will draw a black line for the previous day's high and low on my 1-hour EURUSD chart.

  - *Optimal entry/exit levels.* I will show, side by side, three EURUSD charts to identify the optimal entry/exit levels: the 15-minute chart, the 1H chart, and the 4-hour chart.

- **TRADE ENTRY POINT.** To determine the ideal trade entry point, I will follow these steps:

- To set an entry for a *buy* trade, I will look for the ideal entry point within 5 pips of the M2 line or at the same level as the previous day's low, whichever is about 40 to 50 pips below the pivot line. In the best-case scenario, I will place my *buy* entry level near or at the S1 line (which should be approximately 80 pips below the pivot line).

- If I contemplate a *sell* trade, I will generally look for the ideal entry point within 5 pips of the M3 line or 5 to 10 pips below the previous day's high, whichever is about 40 to 50 pips above the pivot line. In the best-case scenario, I will place my *sell* trade near or at the R1 line (which should be approximately 80 pips above the pivot line).

- I will try hard to pick entry points that work around important price barriers, so that they shield my stop losses (see the following discussion) and never block the EURUSD from reaching my profit target.

- I realize that picking the right trade entry point is one of the most important factors determining trade success. This skill may not come easily at first, but by following this trading plan, I will be right much more often than I am wrong.

- **STOP-LOSS LEVEL.** As a rule of thumb, I will place my stop-loss level <u>30</u> pips above my trade entry price. I will keep in mind that the important price barriers I've identified can work on my favor as a line of defense, keeping the EURUSD from hitting my stop loss, if:

  - My stop-loss level is 15 to 20 pips above the price barrier in a *sell* EURUSD situation.

  - My stop-loss level is 15 to 20 pips below the price barrier in a *buy* EURUSD situation.

- **PROFIT TARGET.** As a rule of thumb, I will place my profit target **40 to 42 pips** away from my entry-level point. I will pick trade entry points that will not require EURUSD to cross a major price barrier to reach my profit target. If I see that my **40-pip** profit objective could be hindered by a major price barrier, I will evaluate whether the trade is worth taking at the entry price level I envisioned and maybe not take it at all.

- **CONTINGENCIES.** If I begin my pretrade analysis after GMT 00:00, it is quite possible that I may have missed a trading opportunity. No matter at what time I begin this process, I commit to analyzing objectively whether I can still follow the basic rules in my trading plan. If there are indications that the pivot challenge has taken place and I missed the ideal trade entry, I will note this in my trade journal and look for new opportunities tomorrow.

PLACING THE TRADE

- If my pretrade analysis identified a trading opportunity, I will place a trade using one of the following methods:

  □ *Buy limit order.* In situations in which Rule 1 applies and I believe that the EURUSD will drop to my ideal entry price before it jumps in value, I will place a *buy* limit pending order following the steps seen in Figure 7-6. I will make sure to include stop-loss and take-profit levels. After I receive confirmation that the order is in place, I can check either after a few hours or the next day to see the results of my pending order.

  □ *Sell limit order.* In situations in which Rule 2 applies and I believe the EURUSD will rise to my ideal entry price before it drops in value, I will place a *sell* limit pending order following the steps seen in Figure 7-6. After I receive confirmation that the order has been placed, I can check either after a few hours or the next day to see the results of my pending order.

☐ *Market order.* If I completed my pretrade analysis and the EURUSD happens to be at or very close to my ideal entry-level price, I will place a market order at the prevailing prices. After the order is in effect, I will edit my order to add a stop-loss level and a take-profit level. As soon as I add these prices, I can check either after a few hours or the next day to see the results of my market order.

MONITORING THE TRADE

- Monitoring a pending trade is not required but could enhance my weekly results. As I check the status of my pending order 1 to 2 hours after placing it, I will cancel my pending order if it has not been filled and I've reason to believe the pivot challenge has already occurred. This type of monitoring can help me avoid unnecessary losses on unfilled limit orders.

TRADE FREQUENCY

- I will place up to **one** trade per day until I learn other strategies that open up new solid trading opportunities.
- If I am bored and feel the urge to trade *something* or to try variations of the strategy, I will use demo account 2. Demo account 1 will not be used for experimentation.

TRADE DURATION

- The trade duration will be determined by market conditions, but will generally be **only a few hours** and always **less than one day.**

- I will cancel an inactive limit order prematurely only if I see that the pivot line has been crossed or if I suspect that the pivot challenge for the day has already taken place.
- If a limit order goes unfilled by the time the new GMT 00:00 comes around, I will cancel the order.
- If I am in an order at the time the new GMT 00:00 comes around and I have not reached my profit target or stop loss, I will close the trade manually.

CHARTS

- I will have several candlestick charts open in MT4 tracking changes in EURUSD. I will use them primarily during the pretrade evaluation process, but I will also use them to check and see if there has been unusual trading activity that rattles the mood or general price direction.
  - □ *15-minute chart.* I will install the VaraTrade Pivot Lines indicator on this chart. This, the most active chart in my platform, is where I can see EURUSD trading within important lines, such as the blue pivot, M2/S1, and M3/R1 lines. Optional indicators to have on this chart include 20-period Bollinger bands, a 40-period SMA, and a 20-period SMA.
  - □ *1-hour chart.* This chart provides an intermediate outlook of that found in shorter-term (15-minute) and longer-term (4-hour) charts. I will add important price barriers on this chart (multicolored horizontal lines). I will also add a green 40-period SMA, a red 80-period SMA, and 21-period Bollinger bands. Each day, I will try to remove horizontal lines that are no longer relevant to keep my chart from getting too crowded.

□ *4-hour chart.* This chart has three SMA lines (20-, 40-, and 80-period), Bollinger bands (20-period), and relevant Fibonacci levels. Generally, if the EURUSD price is above the 80-period SMA, the trend is rising. Conversely, if the price for EURUSD is below the 80-period SMA, the trend is falling. This chart can be transformed into a daily and weekly chart to find longer-term support and resistance lines that do not appear in short-term charts. When a candle closes on the 4-hour chart, the signals are more reliable than those on the 1-hour or 15-minute charts.

TRADE JOURNAL

- I will take 10 minutes at the end of each day to keep a log of my trading activity, and I will take 5 to 10 minutes at the start of each trading session to review my notes. I will use either a web-based trading log or a simple notebook next to my computer. The purpose of the trading journal is to create a log of what is most meaningful during each trading session: what I learned, what surprised me, what I find easy and hard about my trading plan, and questions that I should ask my trading coach (if I have one) when I see her.

MENTAL CONDITIONING

- I recognize that mental conditioning is as important as having a sound trading strategy.
- I have made a point of shaving emotional highs and lows while trading, so that a 60- to 70-pip profit will not make me very excited and a 30-pip loss will not upset me much.

- I learn from my mistakes and will stay clear of "regret traps" where a person becomes obsessed about what he should have done differently.
- I recognize that hindsight (looking at the past from the present) is cruel and unfair. As a result, I will stand by my carefully analyzed trading decisions.
- I embrace an attitude of cautious optimism, avoiding overconfidence and self-defeating impulses.
- I derive more satisfaction from following the rules in my trading plan than from positive trading results that came about by breaking the rules.
- Likewise, I feel calm in the face of losses that came about despite my having followed all the rules in my plan, including having a good trade entry.
- Trading forex should be a fun and rewarding experience. Whenever I feel tempted to spend longer hours than I agreed to in the trading plan, I will have the wisdom to pull away and keep a healthy balance in life.
- I get a huge satisfaction boost from a steady string of 30- to 40-pip gains, although I probably could have earned much more if I had set a larger (riskier) take-profit level.

ACCOUNT SAFEGUARDS

- I realize that the road to becoming a disciplined trader is bumpy, sometimes unpaved, and not in a straight line. I will make mistakes along the way!
- If I put myself in a situation where I am in an emotionally charged state after a loss greater than **30 pips,** I will close the trading platform and give myself a **two-day** vacation from trading.

- I will stay clear of the emotional roller coaster that comes from doing "revenge trading" (trying to make up what I lost, often by risking even more).
- If I do well on a demo account over time but fail to carry that performance over to a live account, I will consider hiring a trading coach or going back to a demo account *if* my live trading account losses equal **20 percent** of my original balance.

ADDITIONAL PROTECTIVE MEASURES

- I will install the MT4 trading platform on two or more computers or mobile devices, each set up with my account details. This will minimize the risk that a hardware or virus problem in one of the computers will prevent me from trading when I need to. I will try to have two or more ways to access the Internet from home, maybe using my home Internet and my smartphone.
- I will have my broker's phone number on my mobile speed dial in case I need to edit or close a trade that is either open or pending in situations in which I can't access my trading platform in the normal way. I will also keep my account numbers handy in my phone so that I can solve trading issues easily. My live account number(s) is (are): _____, _____, and _____.

Mental Conditioning

I trust that you are excited about what you have learned so far and that you are feeling increasingly ready to trade the forex market. Now I want to give you some mental conditioning training that not many traders have had.

The reason why a whole chapter is devoted to this is that establishing a significant positive change in our lives—like trading for a living—takes a concerted effort that aligns our habits, thought patterns, feelings, and goals.

It does us no good to spend a few hundred or a few thousand dollars on high-quality forex education and to develop a very positive attitude if our nonconscious brain ends up sabotaging the whole experience so that we don't achieve the desired results. Our brain sabotages good goals we set for ourselves *all the time!*

Therefore, this chapter will teach you what I have learned about how the mind works and how you could have a better chance of incorporating the new principles that you've learned from this book.

THE MIND'S POWER TO ACCEPT OR REJECT CHANGE

Throughout this book, and especially in Chapter 8, I have referred to self-defeating thought patterns and strong negative emotions, such as fear and greed. To harness the impact from these emotions, we will discuss how the mind controls processes and largely determines outcomes.

The mind can be split in numerous ways, but I'd like to focus on a simple division: your conscious mind and your nonconscious mind. Your ability to think in the now, set goals, and use your imagination is what we understand as the conscious mind—and it's the ruler of the brain, right? Wrong.

The nonconscious mind is infinitely more powerful than the conscious brain, but things get done when the two sides work together.

Much of what I will discuss in this chapter I learned from John Assaraf, a truly remarkable man. For those of you who do not know John that well, he is an entrepreneur and an acclaimed author. He launched four multimillion-dollar businesses, including the RE/MAX franchise for the state of Indiana, with revenues of more than $6 billion. He also runs PraxisNow (praxisnow.com), a research and development firm that creates some of the most powerful evidence-based brain-training tools and programs in the world. John wrote an internationally bestselling book, *Having It All,* and was one of the key participants in the hit DVD and book *The Secret.*

Clearly, during his life, John Assaraf has learned principles that are worth sharing. Some of his life mentors and inspirations were Bob Proctor, Earl Nightingale, and Napoleon Hill. The part of John's work that made the biggest impact on me has been *The Answer,* a book that he coauthored with Murray Smith (Simon & Schuster, 2008). The book is a breathtaking journey into the human mind and human potential. The first half of the book reveals the passion that John has for understanding the connection between thoughts and reality.

The research he shares with the reader is vast and credible. The book starts with the old (Cartesian) view that spiritual things and material things are separate, then continues all the way to breakthroughs based on quantum science that reveal a provoking connection between thoughts and the physical world. Rather than do the subject an injustice by cutting the explanation too short, I will focus on the parts that made the most sense to me as a person and as a trader:

- We live in a world in which there are written and unwritten rules about us and about others. These rules control how we see the world and our place in it. For example, we think of ourselves in terms of our job, as what we do: plumbers, financial analysts, or whatever. We also think of ourselves in terms of our nationality, our gender, our age, and other such factors.
- For the past 50 or 60 years, the traditional path to financial stability has appeared to be: finish high

school, go to college, get a "job," work for 40 or more years, then somehow "retire" and enjoy the last 10 to 30 years of your life.

- Careers in trading or entrepreneurship are viable routes for financial stability, but our minds are not readily equipped to adopt them—we have to go out of our way to teach our mind how a trading lifestyle can help us achieve our life's goals.

- Our environment also helps shape our perception of what amount of money we are worth, what we are capable of producing in a month or a year. This very worrisome perception of us as making, say, $50,000 a year prevents us from thinking and doing what will help us produce $65,000 or $200,000 a year. Perception (whether conscious or unconscious) determines reality.

- There are agents of change all around us (marriage, children, a new home, divorce, the passing of a loved one, high unemployment, job insecurity, or an inability to meet financial obligations) that tell us that something is wrong with the traditional path to financial stability that we have adopted. But the ingrained patterns of thought in our minds cling desperately to what we have done in the past, even if it does not solve our financial problems.

- Even people who react to agents of change and wish to break out of a negative lifestyle cycle often struggle to reach a better future. For example, on New Year's Day, many people set a goal of being fit by spring but abandon that goal before February. Or, what about the people who start a restaurant or launch a business without enough preparation, only to see it fail within a year?

- But there *are* people who look and find what they were looking for. There *are* people who understand how change is realized, how goals are set, and what intermediate steps should be taken. These individuals define and visualize their desired life in great detail. These are the lucky ones who persisted or tumbled upon the right help to achieve a more fulfilling life.

JOHN ASSARAF'S NEURAL RECONDITIONING PROCESS

In my opinion, John Assaraf's process for realizing change, something that he calls the Neural Reconditioning Process, is the most complete perspective on realizing positive change that *sticks*.

Goal setting happens on the cognitive side of the brain, and it has been proved that this process fails to produce lasting change unless the nonconscious brain is also "recalibrated" to embrace, or at least not sabotage, the new goal. I will list the steps in this powerful process as they appear in *The Answer*.

Step 1. Create a new vision of your financial and business success. Make it emotionally rich and crystal clear.

Step 2. Create powerful declarations and affirmations that support that new vision.

Step 3. Develop emotional anchors for neural linking.

Step 4. Prepare a portfolio of imprinting material, which may include written, auditory, visual, and subliminal pieces.

Step 5. Maintain a brief daily routine of reconditioning techniques, three times a day (upon waking, at midday, and before bed).

Step 6. Employ various forms of neurotechnology to reinforce these images throughout the day.

I recommend that the reader evaluate John Assaraf's detailed explanations of this critical six-step process of change.

Why do we go to the trouble of putting these steps into practice? Couldn't we just *decide* to become successful traders?

The answer is no. Have you heard this riddle? Six frogs are sitting on a big lotus leaf, and one of them decides to jump; how many frogs are left on the leaf? If you answered five, you are with the majority. But the correct answer is six. Just because one frog *decided* to jump does not mean that it jumped. Our minds are prone to believe that we do things that we decide to do.

Our brain is wired in a certain way, and the steps just given are carefully calibrated to bypass the mind's natural defenses against change.

In particular, there are two parts of our nonconscious mind that we need to bring into collaboration with our conscious mind: the reticular activating system and the psycho-cybernetic mechanism.

The *reticular activating system* (RAS) processes everything that you see, hear, feel, taste, or smell. It prevents your conscious brain from being overwhelmed by the terabytes of information that our senses are picking up every instant. It filters out information that *it* considers irrelevant or unnecessary. But wait a second. Did you ever take the time to program your RAS to tell it what to filter out and what to alert you to? You didn't do this consciously, but you did it indirectly.

One way in which the RAS is at work, even while we are asleep, is illustrated by a nursing mother who, when she is asleep, tunes out loud noises from cars and cats outside the house, but wakes up if she hears her baby give a soft cry or hears a noise that could have come from the baby's room.

The flip and troubling side of the RAS is that it focuses your attention on what you persistently think about. If your thoughts are on what people have done to you, or on the idea that you can't earn more than $70,000 a year, then your RAS will find and highlight situations that will prove that you are correct about those worries. In other words, its filtering mechanism will reinforce what you think about and what you are passionate about.

The *psycho-cybernetic mechanism*, or *set point*, is a machinelike control-and-response mechanism within our brain. The set point controls functions such as body temperature, weight, and other forms of homeostasis. The role of the set point is to return our body to a situation of nondanger or normality.

For example, when our body temperature gets above normal, the response from the set point is to sweat and thus try to decrease the body temperature. When we step onto a road without looking and mechanically put a foot on the street, the set point instinctively sends a rush of epinephrine to the right part of the brain within milliseconds, causing us to step back away from danger.

The role of the set point is necessary and generally quite good, but sometimes it interferes when we want to change our life from a negative normal to a new positive normal.

When people set a goal of learning something new, whether it is learning to trade or to drive or to diet, our set point stands ready to flood our brain with chemicals that create anxiety over the changes associated with those things that we are learning.

John Assaraf also addresses the issue of our having financial set points. I am willing to bet that most people reading this paragraph right now have a well-ingrained belief that there is no way you can increase your income fivefold within two years. That unspoken belief is an indication that you have a financial set point that suggests that earning such an income would not be normal or attainable for you.

And this is key. As you start to adopt a trading lifestyle, your set point may trigger an alert because the monthly return that you are aiming for is around 10 to 15 percent, a rate of return that your brain has been taught to believe can be achieved only over a year's time (if you are lucky), and only if your money is invested prudently by experts. Not surprisingly, the yellow flags go up because potentially earning this kind of return is not normal.

It is very true that in any given day, you could well lose 1 percent, and this is a just reason for the set point to step in and say, "Watch out." But, we have to realize that the risk of loss does not have to paralyze us and prevent us from trading. After all, we don't stop driving because there is a real chance that a sleepy or distracted driver may slam into our car one day.

As drivers we take measures to minimize the risk of accidents, and as traders you would do well to heed all the risk-management guidelines in this book. So, the key things that we need to teach our set point are that (1) trading with caution should not raise yellow or red flags in our mind, and (2) it is OK to make much more money trading than we normally make from our other activities.

THE POWER OF FOCUS

What happens when I tell you, "*Don't* look at this black dot"?   •

You look for the black dot. Most of you would, anyhow. Our ability to focus is powerful, and it usually does not pay attention to words like *don't*, *no*, or *except*. Our reticular activating system operates that way, focusing on things that we feel strongly about.

What is a good focus to have when you start trading currencies? Winning trades. Thinking you are one of the luckiest traders in the world. It should be as if every time you get in front of the computer, the right trading opportunities are just there, and you take them. You feel great about yourself because you have learned the right trading rules. You are grateful for the training, and you are grateful for the ease with which you are building a steady forex income.

Now answer this. What might happen if you let negative feelings (fear, inadequacy, or suspicion) be the focus of your thoughts? Then the ride would be completely different. You would send a different message to your RAS. The RAS would start finding negative things in your trading to prove that your fears are justified, that you were not born for this, and other sad excuses why this does not work for you. Over a short period, your financial set point would start to send chemicals to your brain that would try to steer you back to a more normal life, a life without trading—but perhaps a normal life that does not really make you happy or does not inspire you.

I am grateful for the losses that I have experienced in live trading. Those few instances have allowed me to empathize with all of my fellow traders, and to understand what it's like to face a setback in our road to financial success. I am happy that I realized that my mistakes do not define me and that my lack of discipline for a period did not determine whether I could become a successful trader.

To me, finding good trading opportunities is like finding parking spaces close to where I am going. If you ask my wife, she will tell you that I am the luckiest guy when it comes to finding the parking spots that everybody wants, close to the door of wherever we are going. My mindset is that I *will* find a parking spot near where I want it. I don't know in what row, I just know that one will be already open or will open up within 15 seconds of when I get to where I am going. And it happens more than 90 percent of the time when I go to Target or Walmart. I started believing this as a fun test of a DVD that I watched about two or three years ago. I don't have a logical reason why it happens, but I have come to believe that anything I do could be replicated by anyone who sets her mind to it.

THE 30-DAY TRADER RECONDITIONING PLAN

By now, you have enough background on trading and the workings of the mind to join me in creating a 30-day reconditioning plan to become a currency trader. We could think of this plan as applying the principles of John Assaraf's Neural Reconditioning Process to forex trading.

Step 1. Create a new vision of your financial and business success. Make it emotionally rich and crystal clear.

John Assaraf clarifies that "you have to be 100% clear on what you want to achieve." Olympic athletes take time to visualize the perfect race, all the way up to where someone is placing a gold medal around their neck. The clearer your vision is, the better the chance you have to achieve it. The following is a sample declaration from John (adapted slightly by me).[1] You will it read daily and picture it in ever-greater detail—no matter how distant this reality might seem from your reality today:

> Today my net worth is _____. I am now earn-
> ing _____ a year from my trading activity and my
> work, and I am saving _____ per year after taxes.
> Money is flowing to me in abundance. I am joyfully giving
> 10 percent of my income to my favorite charities, and another
> 10 percent to my church. Life at the summit is sweet and
> satisfying.
>
> I am living the life of my dreams. Love, laughter, and
> unbridled passion fuel my life and turn my dreams into real-
> ity. I am grateful for my vibrant health and high energy, and
> for the health and happiness of my spouse and children. My
> family and I grow closer and wiser every day, sharing joy and
> possibility with all those we love and care for. My heart and
> my head are soaring with possibility and opportunity. I am
> blessed and grateful for my whole life and everything in it.

Step 2. Create powerful declarations and affirmations that support that new vision.

Step 1 sends a very powerful message to your noncon-scious mind. Now we need to make sure that your everyday actions mirror your goal. Powerful affirmations are ways in which we steer ourselves back into the road that leads to our goal.

One of your affirmations could be something like: "I believe in necessary rest and in being engaged in uplifting activities." Anytime you stay a bit too long on a couch, this affirmation springs back to life to help you find the strength to get up off the couch and take positive action. If you don't, then you are sending mixed signals to your nonconscious mind.

John tells us that the key to writing positive affirmations is that they "must be bold, clear, positive, and stated in the present tense."[2]

Here are some affirmations that will help you in your trading:

- I find the right trading opportunities without effort.
- I am absolutely certain of my ability to generate any amount of trading income I choose.
- I have the right life experiences and background to succeed in trading currencies online.
- I am one of the luckiest traders in the world.
- I make the right trading decisions at the right time.

Step 3. Develop emotional anchors for neural linking.

An affirmation that is associated with (or linked to) a feeling is memorable and powerful. When we ask someone what she was doing on a given morning, she might struggle and not be able to remember. What if we asked a person what he was doing on the morning of September 11, 2001—the day of the terrorist attack on the New York World Trade Center?

Most people would remember exactly what they were doing when they heard the news. Strong emotions cause us to remember specific moments.

What John Assaraf has also found is that remembering the positive, happy feelings of a past moment (a business triumph, the birth of a child, the day of a marriage) can be associated not just with a day in the past but with a present-day affirmation.

The first thing to do is to remember in as much detail as possible how you felt when you accomplished something you are proud of, then write down those thoughts as best you can:

> The birth of my first child. I remember the struggle of my sweetie. I was holding her hand. Then, so quickly, that anxiety I felt was replaced with a knot in my throat and an overwhelming feeling of happiness to see this beautiful baby spring to life. What a rush!

Once we have brought out this feeling and reopened the neural pathways, we imprint in our mind the affirmation that we are looking to link. We do this by simply restating our affirmation while we are still *under the effects* of this powerful, positive emotion.

After you relive the birth of your first child, for example, you think, "I find the right trading opportunities without effort." This step is as simple as that.

Step 4. Prepare a portfolio of imprinting material, which may include written, auditory, visual, and subliminal pieces.

By the time a person is 17 years old, she has heard, "No, you can't" an average of 150,000 times. And she has heard, "Yes, you can" about 5,000 times.[3] So it should be no surprise that our nonconscious mind needs all the help it can get to overcome years of believing that *we probably can't do things*.

This portfolio of imprinting material is made up of imagery, sounds, and smells so that our senses can create a more real image of what we are looking for, our goals and affirmations.

In the portfolio, we can include written statements, audio recordings, or vision boards with pictures that depict our goals. I recommend having a vision board and including a trading statement that shows your trading account having a bigger balance than what you start out with, such as $75,000, and bank account and pension account statements with even larger balances.

Step 5. Maintain a brief daily routine of reconditioning techniques, three times a day (upon waking, at midday, and before bed).

I have to admit that the change of pattern involved in this step was not easy to make, but it has been really worth it. Your nonconscious mind will turn the corner and start helping you achieve your goals once it has accumulated enough information about the *new normal* that you are looking for.

John Assaraf recommends establishing a routine at the times of day when our nonconscious is most susceptible to reprogramming: shortly after waking up, in the midafternoon, and as we get ready to go to bed. During these times, our body is tired and our mind is not fully alert.

This step calls for us finding a quiet spot (ideally the same spot each time, at the same time) where we follow an established meditation routine. The length of this routine can be as little as 30 minutes per day—about 10 minutes per session.

- Turn off your phone, get away from the computer, and close the door to avoid distractions and minimize loud noises in the environment.
- Sit quietly and comfortably in a chair or on the floor; hold your hands any way you like.
- In that relaxed sitting position, close your eyes and take a slow deep breath through your nose, letting the air out through your mouth.
- Focus. This first part of the routine is to enhance the ability of your frontal lobe to focus for five minutes, initially on one single thing at a time. You start by focusing on the base of your nostrils and the air flowing through them.
- As your mind begins to wander in all directions, you gently bring it back to the focus on the base of your nostrils as many times as necessary. What matters most is that you exercise your mind's ability to focus. Be patient with yourself.
- After about two weeks, extend your meditation time to 15 minutes. After another two weeks, if you can, extend it to 30 minutes.

- It is important that you do this every day. If you miss a day, it is OK. Resume the following day and pick up where you left off. There is no sense in feeling like a failure because you missed a day.

What I have described so far is the meditation component of the routine. What comes next is the neural reconditioning part of the routine.

After the focus exercise, you begin a few minutes of visualization of your financial and trading success described in Step 1. For example, you close your eyes and picture yourself looking at a trading statement for the past three months and feeling the excitement of seeing a trading performance of 20 percent per month. You experience a sense of wonder at how it all happened even though this is all so new to you. You imagine yourself bragging a little in front of friends and colleagues, and you feel a real sense of hope that your trading activities will lead to a more plentiful retirement and lifestyle. The focus exercise has empowered you to be able to generate with your mind a new reality, in great detail. The first few times you practice this, it will feel contrived and silly. That is OK. With every time you do it, the vision of your new normal will take on a life of its own. You are effectively reprogramming your financial set point and enabling your reticular activating system to get to work at making this new vision a reality.

You can also add sounds, tactile sensations, and smells to create this vision that with every meditation session becomes more and more real.

Conclude your meditation routine by recalling powerful positive events in your life and reading a laminated sheet with your affirmations, thus creating a powerful linkage that your nonconscious mind learns to recognize as something good and desirable.

Step 6. Employ various forms of neurotechnology to reinforce these images throughout the day.

This step refers to adopting subtle forms of mental reconditioning. It refers to using sounds and even software that sends subliminal messages to your nonconscious mind without distracting your conscious mind.

This step could be as simple as softly playing a sound file with your recorded affirmations while you are doing work or repetitive tasks.

Trading Resources

I've scoured the web looking for trader sites of substance, and especially for those precious few that make an effort to be visually appealing. This chapter goes over my top picks of services and websites for forex traders.

E-MAIL SIGNALS

E-mail signals serve a purpose, but they have to be used carefully. That purpose is to help people who lack the confidence, skill, or time to spot trading opportunities. I would caution anyone using e-mail signals to (1) become familiar with the trading strategy from which the signals are generated, (2) understand the risk and reward that the signal provider typically incorporates into the e-mail signals, and (3) feel confident about the quality of the signals. As always, try the e-mail signals on a demo account before you ever try them on a real account.

VaraTrade.com. In Chapter 3, I said that the three elements of a great trader education are knowledge, tools, and support. This book has given you the trading knowledge (strategy, risk management, and a trading plan) and has made available a VT Pivot Indicator that is one of the tools you will need. VaraTrade also provides the support component. A VaraTrade senior analyst takes a daily look at the VT Pivot Roadmap strategy and sends out an e-mail with trading ideas. I recommend that you consider getting this service, particularly if you are not sure how to implement the strategy or if you are not getting the results you are looking for. The service is called VaraTrade Daily FX Signals. There is a 14-day free trial, after which $49 a month gives you access to the daily signal and the VT Pivot Indicator.

RTS-Forex.com. Rockefeller Treasury Services (RTS Forex) is operated by Barbara Rockefeller, a stellar trader and technical analyst. I have interacted professionally with Barbara and feel very comfortable referring her to others, particularly to intermediate and advanced traders. Her multiyear profitable track record of issuing actionable trade ideas is quite an accomplishment. She offers subscribers a superb daily morning briefing summarizing the main points in the financial press that relate to trading major currency pairs—something that I believe is well worth the annual subscription.

Collective2.com. Collective2 offers signals based on hundreds of trading strategies. The website gives you plenty of information that allows you to evaluate each signal provider. Just be sure you understand the trading strategy and test the performance on a demo account. If it is successful, implement it with a small live account. There are free signals and others that cost $100 per month or more.

FOREX NEWS

It's clear that reading forex news daily is an essential part of trading. What is less clear, however, is how to find the best, most relevant news in one place. With the number of journalists at major newspapers decreasing, news desks cannot possibly cover all the topics that are needed in detail. However, by combining a few reputable newspapers, readers can get a more thorough view of what's happening in the world.

VaraTrade.com. What I like about the VaraTrade news section is that news comes from more than 150 reputable news feeds that VaraTrade has handpicked and that each user can combine (aggregate). Registered VaraTrade users can select precise news feeds (for free) from 25 news categories, such as the U.S. dollar, the economy, and Asia. Some of the news providers include FXStreet.com, DailyFX.com, Seeking Alpha, ForexFactory.com, the *Financial Times*, CNN, the *New York Times*, *The Economist*, the BBC, and the *Wall Street Journal* (all of the feeds offer free previews, though a few feeds require a separate subscription to read the full story).

News.Google.com. Google News is much better at aggregating news content than Yahoo! or Microsoft. The process of choosing news that is relevant to traders is doable, but complex—you have to know what news feed to look for. The levers to show the frequency of a topic or news source are very useful.

ForexLive.com. The website ForexLive.com is run by a team of very experienced journalists who know the type of news that is important to traders. The service is free and very insightful.

Twitter. If you have never tried Twitter, it is worth exploring. I didn't "get" Twitter until late 2011, but I am now a heavy user. Twitter allows the rapid spread of user comments and important news links. You pick whom to follow based on how much value their tweets generate or how much they resonate with you. The great thing about Twitter is that you can read about developing stories before they get to press. In addition, I think Twitter is a great way to stay in touch whenever you are on the road and have a few minutes of downtime. I tweet under the name of @ELTRADE about issues that affect online trading and about news stories that catch my eye. I have also built Twitter lists that are dedicated to traders—that is, you can follow me and also any of my public lists. I also post articles that educate traders to my blog, TRADEIQ .BLOGSPOT.COM.

Economic calendar

There are several firms that provide insightful economic calendars:

Myfxbook.com. This great site requires a free registration, but the economic calendar service offers an alarm service that notifies you by e-mail 30 minutes (or whatever time you select) before the event is released.

Econoday.com. This calendar is very complete, free, and used by many financial portals, like Nasdaq.com and IBTimes .com. The premium MyEconoday service ($9.99 per month) creates an economic calendar that is viewable through your mobile device or Microsoft Outlook account and is updated automatically.

Major forex websites. Three forex news sites (FXstreet.com, Forexpros.com, and ForexFactory.com) also offer robust economic calendars.

Trader education methods

Aite Group's research on the U.S. investor market indicates that the most experienced traders take a diverse approach to increasing their trading skills (see Figure 10-1). Active traders (those who place between 3 and 10 trades per month)

FIGURE 10-1 Preferred Methods for Enhancing Trading Skills, U.S. Traders, 2011

Q. As you decide to trade something new or enhance your skill in certain areas you are familiar with, what is your preferred method for learning about online trading topics?

The local office of an investment firm: 14% 24%
Educational material from brokerage firm: 36% 26%
Study books on the subject: 44% 28%
Read blogs and forums: 28% 31%
Online trading room: 25% 36%
Structured course - online: 19% 23%
Structured course - offline: 14% 26%
Webinar: 24% 26%
Seminar: 22% 33%

■ Active traders (n =143, traders who place 3 to 10 trades/month)
▪ More frequent trader (n =77, traders who place more than 10 trades/month)

Source: Aite Group, U.S. Investor Survey, 1,014 participants, December 2011.

gain most of their knowledge from books and also from educational materials provided by their brokers. The more frequent traders (those who place more than 10 trades per month) also value books, but they also like to try a variety of things like attending online trading rooms, seminars, and reading online blogs or forums.

What makes me leery about trader forums in general is that their information is inconsistent, incomplete, and of questionable reliability. You don't know whether someone on the other end has a sound risk-management system in place, or whether he has a complete picture of what he is advising others about. Unfortunately, many people (particularly new traders) lack the proper background to determine whether forum/blog information is valid and appropriate for them.

RECOMMENDED TRADING BOOKS

The following are trading books that are highly acclaimed by connoiseurs and traders. Some are easier to read, while others are more technical. Enhancing your technical analysis ability is necessary if you wish to become better at spotting trading opportunities and identifying market moods based on chart formations. Not all of these books are forex-specific, but what you will learn from them is applicable to forex.

- Stephen Bigalow, *High Candlestick Patterns* (Houston, TX: Profit Publishing, 2005)
- John Bollinger, *Bollinger on Bollinger Bands* (New York: McGraw-Hill, 2002).
- Thomas Bulkowski, *Getting Started in Chart Patterns* (Hoboken, NJ: Wiley, 2006).
- Tushar S. Chande, *Beyond Technical Analysis,* 2nd ed. (Hoboken, NJ: Wiley, 2001).
- Mark Douglas, *Trading in the Zone: Master the Market with Confidence* (New York: New York Institute of Finance, 2001).
- John Murphy, *Technical Analysis of the Financial Markets: A Comprehensive Guide to Trading Methods*

and Applications (New York: New York Institute of
Finance, 1999).

- Steve Nison, *Japanese Candlestick Charting
  Techniques*, 2nd ed. (New York: New York Institute of
  Finance, 2001).
- Steve Nison, *The Candlestick Course* (Hoboken, NJ:
  Wiley, 2003).
- Martin Pring, *Technical Analysis Explained*, 4th ed.
  (New York: McGraw-Hill, 2001),

ONLINE TRADING ROOMS

Online trading rooms are quite effective at providing real-
time support to new traders as they make the transition from
knowing how to trade in theory to knowing how to trade in
real life. After a new trader has learned a trading strategy
theoretically, there is a period of vulnerability during which
she is insecure about how and when to implement her new
knowledge. The main risk during this phase is learning to
trade incorrectly, picking up unproductive habits. Online
trading rooms can work well because they let the trader peek
over the shoulder of the trading coach. A good trading coach

- Identifies in real time what makes a good trade setup
  - Points to trade preconditions that have been met
    or not met
  - Measures risk and reward for a trade
  - Identifies potential trade entry, stop-loss, and
    take-profit levels

- Reminds new traders to exercise patience waiting for the right conditions (e.g., candle close or indicator signal) and not trade prematurely or in excess
- Puts market news in context and shows how the mood of the market is reflected in candle formations
- Shows composure after posting a trade win or loss

Online trading rooms are a relatively new phenomenon, dating back to approximately 2006. These trading rooms are still trying to strike the right balance between the service they are delivering and what they should charge for these services. I've seen very simple trading rooms that charge $20 per month, and I've also seen fancy ones that charge $400 per month—the majority of them are in the price range of $100 to $200 per month.

A few trading room organizations worth evaluating are the following:

fx-Knight.com. The key person behind fx-Knight is Andrei Knight, a well-known figure in forex circles and a regular contributor to large forex websites. His "Pro-Services" include the teaching of high-probability strategies based on Fibonacci studies, pivot points, and moving averages; access to his video library; and, more important, one-hour market briefings twice daily during which he and his team go over the trading opportunities for the next session. The cost is a very reasonable €179 per month.

WinnersEdgeTrading.com. Casey Stubbs leads this team and has been at it since 2007, which is a testament to the value his service has given to traders. Casey "keeps it real," and I believe the business has the right focus—solid strategies, tools, and reliable trading room moderators—so don't be fooled by this firm's simple web design.

Other trading rooms. The price of a good or service often reflects its quality, but sometimes it is driven by higher marketing costs. There are two Australian-based trading rooms that appear to have sound packages for traders but are on the pricier side of the spectrum: LTGGoldRock.com and VertueTrading.com. Both services have trading rooms that remain open 24 hours a day for 5.5 days per week and offer a wider set of strategies and multiple custom indicators. Some trading rooms justify the higher price by promoting a prop-trader program, but this type of program is of questionable value, and I don't recommend it.[1]

ADVANCED TRADING PLATFORMS

In terms of trading platforms, it used to be that each forex brokerage firm would have its own trading platform, and clients would have to learn the trading platform used by their broker. This was annoying because if a client had to change brokers, he would have to learn to use a new trading platform all over again. Today, there are still a lot of single-broker platforms, but a small number of multibroker platforms (MT4, eSignal, Trade Interceptor, Ninja Trader, and a few others) have emerged as the popular alternative. I could never do justice and mention all of the single-broker platforms in this section, so I will just help you to become familiar with a couple of these multibroker platforms.

Trade Interceptor. Trade Interceptor is a new trading platform that is taking forex trading by storm. I would not be surprised if it equaled or exceeded MT4 in popularity a few years from now. It has a strong combination of desktop and mobile platforms. The mobile offering of Trade Interceptor includes four dedicated versions for iPhone, iPad, Android, and Kindle Fire (the iPad version is pictured in Figure 10-2). Each version has abundant technical analysis functionality that lets traders take with them on the road almost as much functionality as they would have on their computer (or multiscreen setup) at home. Trader ratings for its mobile apps in the Android Market and App Store have been off the charts,

FIGURE 10-2 Alternative Trading Platforms, Trade Interceptor for iPad

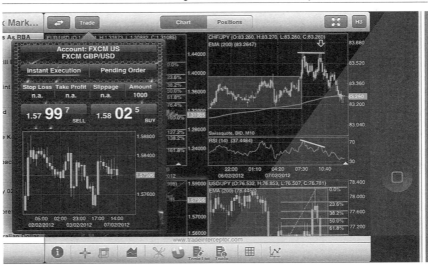

Source: Riflexo.

much higher than the ratings of any other trading platform. Like MT4, Trade Interceptor is free of charge.

eSignal. eSignal has a long tradition of offering advanced trading platforms to sophisticated traders. It offers excellent tools to carry out strategy back-testing. The eSignal platform also stands out for its ability to connect traders to virtually all retail markets: forex, equities, options, futures, fixed income, and index trading. The monthly fee for using this platform is $60 (see Figure 10-3).

FIGURE 10-3 **Alternative Trading Platforms, eSignal Platform**

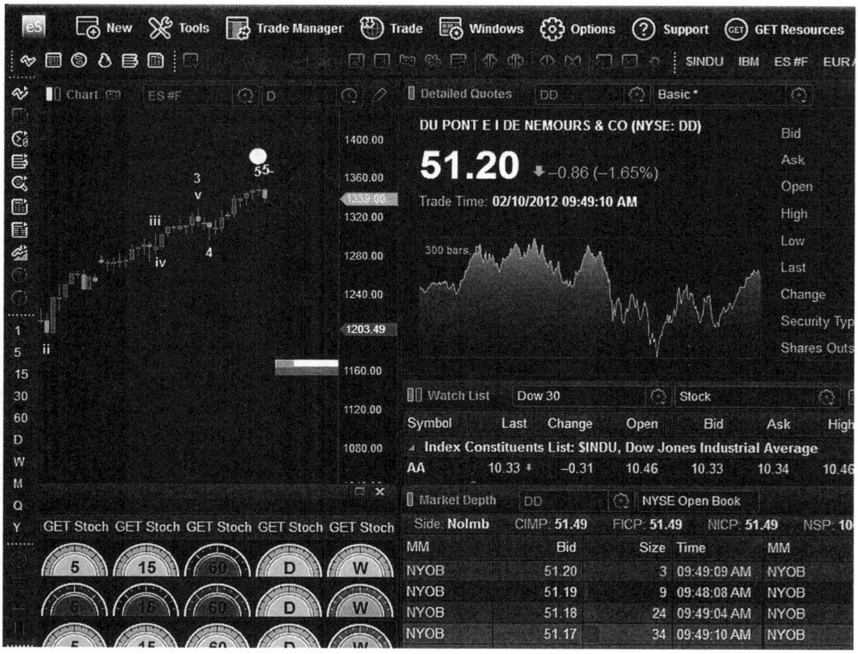

Source: Interactive Data Corporation.

TRADER TOOLS

Many services and technology solutions help traders improve their performance. I recommend readers evaluate the education and tools selection at VaraTrade.com; some are mentioned in this chapter. My favorite trader tool places include

Myfxbook.com. I like Myfxbook.com for various reasons. Once registered (free), a user can connect one or multiple live or demo MT4 accounts to Myfxbook.com and automatically track all activity on these accounts. This information comes in very handy when you are evaluating your trading performance and the risk you are taking. A user can make the information fully public, make it partially public, or keep it all private. My favorite chart to evaluate is "drawdown," which shows how much of our account the user is risking at any time—my recommendation is to keep the maximum drawdown below 5 percent most of the time and never more than 15 percent. I also like the advanced statistics section and the ability to browse through the trade history.

TradeOnTrack.com. TradeOnTrack.com offers a web-based interface with important analytics to help traders be more disciplined. The free version is adequate, and there is a premium version for about $45 per month. The software is a combination of an e-trade journal and trade analytics.

Candlecharts.com. Steve Nison's Candle Highlighter automatically identifies candle formations on various trading platforms (MT4, NinjaTrader, TradeStation, and Trade Navigator), taking out the guesswork for traders. Also, the Product Comparison page is a good place to evaluate the various DVD training courses available.

IBFX.com. I mention IBFX not as the brokerage firm that it is, but because it has an impressive set of free MT4 add-ons for any demo or live account user. Some of these tools include the mini monitor, Candlestick Pattern Recognition (CPR), Autochartist, pip calculator, and Forex Stats. You may use a different broker for your live trading, but you will need to download an IBFX MT4 platform and at least register for a demo account for these indicators to work.

fxTrade.OANDA.com. OANDA is another forex broker that has developed a lot of very useful trader tools. These are found in the OANDA Forex Labs section and include currency correlation, commitment of traders (COT), currency strength heatmap, forex order book, and Forex Trader Statistics. No account needs to be opened and nothing needs to be paid to access these insightful, web-based tools.

TRADER MAGAZINES

A number of excellent publications are available to self-directed traders. All of them contain technical analysis articles and industry developments that are worth knowing about. The magazines that I enjoy reading are

FXTraderMagazine.com. This magazine is free and comes out a few times per year. Its articles abound in substance, are reliable, and can truly improve a trader's knowledge base.

e-Forex.net. *e-Forex* magazine contains insightful articles for retail and institutional audiences involved in forex trading. Four magazines are published yearly for a retail subscription of £175.

FuturesMag.com. *Futures* magazine is one of the most recognizable names in online trading and offers a monthly magazine subscription for $78 per year. There is abundant useful information for free at futuresmag.com, as well as premium content for subscribers.

CurrencyTraderMag.com. *Currency Trader* magazine offers powerful macro and forex charting insights from staff writers and regular contributor Barbara Rockefeller. *Currency Trader* is published monthly and is free, making it a compelling read.

REGULATORY BODIES

The rules and regulations for trading forex vary by country, although not many countries have precise rules for trading forex. Most of the regulators discussed here have issued rules governing retail forex markets for their respective jurisdictions. They stand as rule setters and as arbiters if a trader feels that he has been treated improperly by a regulated broker.

UNITED STATES

Following the passage of the Dodd-Frank Act in 2010, the United States has multiple regulatory bodies that are authorized to regulate the retail forex market: the Commodity Futures Trading Commission (CFTC), the Securities and Exchange Commission (SEC), the Office of the Comptroller of the Currency (OCC), the Federal Deposit Insurance Corporation (FDIC), and the Federal Reserve. Of these, the regulator setting the tone for the forex industry is the CFTC along with its enforcement arm, the National Futures Association (NFA). The various regulators govern the activities of specific types of firms.

- The CFTC regulates introducing brokers (IBs), commodity pool operators (CPOs), commodity trading advisors (CTAs), and forex brokers. Forex brokers are denominated as futures commodity merchants (FCMs) and more precisely as retail foreign exchange dealers (RFEDs). Among other things, the CFTC publishes the financial data of all FCMs on a monthly basis, telling us things like the amount of capital each firm is required to hold and total client funds held. The NFA, in turn, audits FCMs and evaluates traders' complaints as they arise. Firms regulated by the CFTC include 12 or so retail forex firms in the United States: OANDA, FXCM, Gain Capital (FOREX.COM), IBFX, GFT, FXDD, Alpari U.S., and a few others.

- The SEC, in turn, regulates securities exchanges, securities broker-dealer (B/D) firms, investment advisors, and mutual funds. The SEC oversees the activity of more than 4,400 brokerage firms and more than 600,000 registered securities representatives through its enforcement arm, the Financial Industry Regulatory Authority (FINRA). There aren't many securities broker firms authorized to conduct retail forex activities through the SEC, though one of them is Interactive Brokers. There are, however, several high-profile securities B/D firms that offer retail forex to clients while acting as introducing brokers to CFTC-regulated firms. These include E*TRADE, TD Ameritrade/thinkorswim, and Zecco. Charles Schwab is seeking approval to offer retail forex in 2012, possibly through its CFTC-regulated firm optionsXpress.
- The OCC, the FDIC, and the Federal Reserve regulate the U.S. banking sector. These regulatory bodies just announced their retail forex rules in July 2011, so not many banks are known for offering retail forex in the United States just yet. Citibank, through its unit CitiFX Pro, is the exception and has been offering retail forex services to experienced retail traders since 2007. Other banks are also contemplating how to participate in the retail forex market.

It is important for traders to understand the regulatory environment and to help combat fraud and improper business practices. Fraud related to forex and futures activity most often takes the form of individuals posing as successful investment managers (CPOs/CTAs). The fraud takes place when these individuals or small firms ask unsuspecting investors for funds. Once funds are pooled into one account that they control, these fraudsters have the freedom to make improper use of funds, at which point they will go on and forge client statements. Since 2011, it is illegal for any unregistered firm or individual to solicit others to open a forex trading account with a CFTC-regulated FCM. Although each U.S. regulatory body cited here can issue its own retail forex rules, the rules they have issued are largely comparable to those passed by the CFTC, such as maximum leverage set at 50:1.

UNITED KINGDOM

The United Kingdom has a very competent regulator in the Financial Services Authority (U.K. FSA). Its approach to regulating retail forex has been much more laissez-faire (easygoing) than the approaches of other regulators, including the U.S. CFTC, have been. London is the undisputed center of forex trading worldwide, something that has allowed the U.K. FSA to oversee this type of activity from a vantage point of experience. The maximum leverage in the United Kingdom for trading forex is 500:1.

AUSTRALIA

The Australian retail forex market is regulated by the Australian Securities and Investments Commission (ASIC). This is another regulator that has successfully walked the line of having credible regulations and yet having rules that do not stifle retail forex activity. Individuals or firms found guilty of ASIC violations face criminal (not civil) charges. The maximum leverage is 500:1.

SWITZERLAND

The retail forex market in Switzerland had major changes in 2009 and 2010. The country went from having several weak, overlapping regulators in 2007 to having one very stern regulator, the Swiss Financial Market Supervisory Authority (FINMA). In 2010, FINMA required all retail forex brokers to secure a banking license or cease operations. Only a few firms managed to do so, including Swissquotes Bank, Dukascopy Bank, Saxo Bank (Schweiz) AG, and MIG Bank. Swiss firms offer forex trading at a leverage of 100:1.

JAPAN

As mentioned earlier, Japan is the country with the largest number of retail forex traders. The Financial Services Agency (JP FSA) and the Financial Futures Association of Japan (FFAJ) are charged with the task of regulating retail forex activity. There are about 20 medium and large firms offering retail forex in Japan. The maximum leverage has been reduced in two stages: it fell to 50:1 in 2010 and to 25:1 in 2011, where it remains today.

EUROPEAN UNION

The European Union has general securities regulations under the Markets in Financial Instruments (MiFID) directives and has appointed the European Securities and Markets Authority (ESMA) as the region's regulatory coordinator in 2011—there are still national regulators in Europe. As a result, there are no European retail forex regulations other than general trade execution and governance practices under MiFID. Retail forex regulation in continental Europe is very shallow. A lot of MiFID-compliant EU brokers have emerged, but I would venture to say that most of them lack adequate levels of capitalization and operational sophistication because of Europe's weak regulatory oversight in forex matters.

OTHER RESOURCES

Trader events. The main forex trader events in the United States are listed at MoneyShow.com. They include the MoneyShow, World MoneyShow, and Trader Expo events, taking place in Las Vegas, New York City, Chicago, Dallas, and other cities. The classes and the chance to interact with forex brokers and technology vendors make these events very worthwhile.

FX vendor due diligence. There are a few places offering background information about forex vendors. One of these places is ForexPeaceArmy.com, which incidentally used to be called ForexBastards.com. It takes end-user feedback about various kinds of firms, from brokers and educators to trading systems. ForexDatasource.com offers unique ranking information on brokers. I recommend looking for brokers that demonstrate adequate levels of capitalization, have a superior customer service, and show dedication, giving traders the tools they need to succeed.

If you come across a great resource for traders or have had an experience with any of the firms mentioned in this chapter, please let me know—I can be reached by e-mail at javierpaz@me.com.

Maximizing Profitable Trades

I saved this important lesson for the end. So far, I have taught you the optimal conditions for using the VT Pivot Roadmap strategy and how to gain approximately 40 pips per trade while risking up to 30 pips. If you follow the rules strictly as I outline them, I strongly believe that a 65 to 70 percent trade win ratio can be within your reach in as little as a few months.

Let's say you want to know how it is that you can reach your profit goal despite having losses of 30 pips 30 percent of the time. I will use as an example a situation in which you placed 20 trades per month, or roughly one trade per day. Using the ratios described earlier, you would have 6 losing trades out of 20, equivalent to −180 pips (−30 × 6). You would also have 14 profitable trades, for a total of +560 pips (40 × 14). The result would be a net profit of +380 pips (560 − 180), or roughly 95 pips per week.

Let me bring back something that I mentioned in the Introduction:

My definition of a trader's summit is relatively simple but not easy to achieve. It is learning to have more wins than losses, keeping trading losses small, and making profitable trades as large as possible.

This chapter aims to teach you two methods to help you gain more than 40 pips per trade and thus possibly exceed the goal of earning 100 pips per week, net of losses and spread costs.

Method 1: Use of a Trailing Stop

A trailing stop is a common and very handy trading platform tool. It is called a stop because if it is hit, it will stop the trade, and it is "trailing" because it does not remain static in one place like the traditional stop loss. The trailing stop moves in the same direction as a profitable trade. If a trade's floating profit increases 1 pip from (say) 40 pips to 41 pips, the trailing stop also moves 1 pip. And just to clarify, the trailing stop has to be applied manually to an open trade, and when it becomes active, it overrides the previous stop loss.

Two key points about using a trailing stop are when to apply it and how big to make the trailing stop. Rather than spending a lot of time with definitions, I will show you how to attach a trailing stop and provide an example of trailing stops in action. The steps for applying a trailing stop are:

1. Place your mouse over a profitable trade and press the right button of the mouse.

2. As the menu of choices appears, select "Trailing Stop."
3. Then select "Custom."
4. Finally, enter the trailing stop value, such as "200" when the trailing stop is supposed to be 20 pips.

Now I share an example of a trailing stop in action. In Figure 11-1, we revisit what we could have done differently during Day 2 of our eight-day example in Chapter 7. That day, the trading strategy (hypothetically) led me to *sell* EURUSD at 1.3179 with a stop loss at 1.3209 and a fixed profit target of 1.3139. I would consider using a trailing stop when my trade is producing a profit of no less than 30 pips. Most often, I aim for a minimum profit of 40 pips before I apply a trailing stop, and when I do apply it, I set the size of the trailing stop at 20 to 30 pips.

Here is what we could have done differently. Let's say that we entered into the *sell* EURUSD trade at 1.3179. We would apply the trailing stop at 1.3137, 42 pips "in the money" (40 pips minimum profit plus 2 pips spread cost). If you look at the graph in Figure 11-1, 1.3137 is right below the pivot line. If we set a trailing stop of 20 pips, the stop loss would move from the original stop loss of 1.3209 to 1.3157 (1.3137 plus 20 pips).

So what happens when you apply a trailing stop to a profitable *sell* EURUSD trade?

- If the EURUSD goes down further, our potential profit increases. By the time the euro drops to 1.3107,

FIGURE 11-1 Trailing Stop Scenario 1, Favorable Breakout

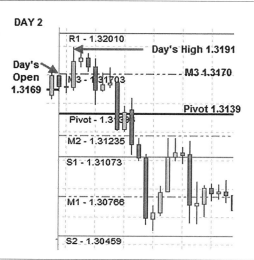

our trade shows a floating profit of 70 pips and our trailing stop has moved down 30 pips to 1.3127. The trailing stop is now locking in a profit of 50 pips (1.3179 minus 1.3127, minus the spread). By the time the euro hits the day's low of 1.3051, our trade shows a cool floating profit of 126 pips, and it also shows our trailing stop at 1.3071, locking in a profit of 106 pips. This trade, like all parties, eventually comes to an end. After hitting the day's low, the euro heads higher, and our trailing stop is triggered at 1.3071. *We are out of the trade with a profit of 106 pips.*

- If the EURUSD had bottomed at M2 (1.3123) and then risen to M3 (1.3170), for example, then our trailing stop would have been triggered without earning

40 pips. If the bottom of the move had been 1.3123, then the trailing stop would have moved down from 1.3157 to 1.3143. *Our final profit would have been 34 pips* (1.3179 minus 1.3143 minus the spread).

When we apply a stop loss, we enter a new risk/reward scenario. As shown in this example, maybe we end up with two or three times the 40 pips we anticipated, or maybe we end up with half of the 40 pips that we originally targeted.

> **KEY CONCEPT:** Setting a trailing stop puts some of the profit we are realizing at risk in exchange for the possibility that we might dramatically increase a trade's profitability.

So when do we use a 30-pip trailing stop? Using a trailing stop higher than 20 pips is riskier, and I would recommend that you try it only after you are more familiar with the operation of trailing stops. There is a basic trade-off when you use wider trailing stops: on the one hand, you risk a bigger portion of your current profit; on the other hand, you may have a better chance to stay in a trade that scores a large gain. If you have a 20-pip trailing stop, it is quite possible that your trade will experience turbulence and get closed before the big move takes place.

Another big factor to consider is picking the "right" trade entry level and the level at which you attach the trailing stop. The VT Pivot Roadmap Strategy gives a precise time to pick an ideal trade entry. When to use a trailing stop and at what levels to attach it, however, are subjective decisions that are best learned with time and practice. If you need help gauging good entry levels, you may benefit from the daily VaraTrade signal e-mails. A sample e-mail might be something like

Minimum distance test: Pass   Mood test: Pass

The pivot strategy for today tells me to BUY EURUSD. I will do so at 1.3045, with a 1.3015 stop loss, 1.3090 initial target, 20 pip trailing stop, 40% trade size.

To clarify this signal, a person could mimic the signal and place a *buy limit* order at 1.3045 with a 1.3015 stop loss. If EURUSD rises to the initial target (1.3090), the trader can apply manually a 20-pip trailing stop if she wants to go beyond the initial 40- to 45-pip profit target. It goes without saying that applying a trailing stop requires the trader to be watching the trade. The 40 percent trade size in the e-mail signal is just an indication that the signal provider is not using the full 1.0 percent in the pivot strategy trade. So if a trader's normal trade size is 3 mini lots, then 40 percent of that would be 1.2 mini lots.

I conclude this section with an important observation about trailing stops. When you set a firm stop loss, it is saved in the trade server of your forex broker. But when you set a trailing stop, it is saved only in your computer (that is, your forex broker does not know about it until the signal to close a trade is received). What this also means is that *if you put to sleep (suspend or hibernate) the computer on which your trading platform resides, then any trailing stop that is open will stop updating—and thus it may not exit a trade when you expect it to!* For the trailing stop to work properly, your computer needs to be active and connected to the Internet. Be aware that sometimes machines go to sleep automatically after a period of inaction.

METHOD 2: USE OF STAGGERED ORDERS

In addition to the use of trailing stops, I make use of staggered orders to achieve more than 40 pips. I use this method when I don't have the inclination to wait and apply a trailing stop. As the name suggests, this strategy calls for using more than one order and profit targets that are staggered. Let's say we use a set of three staggered trades for a given day. The staggered-order setup could look like this:

- *Trade 1. Sell* EURUSD at 1.3120 with a 1.3150 stop loss and a 1.3080 take profit (40 pips), 40 percent of normal trade size.
- *Trade 2. Sell* EURUSD at 1.3120 with a 1.3150 stop loss and a 1.3070 take profit (50 pips), 20 percent of normal trade size.
- *Trade 3. Sell* EURUSD at 1.3120 with a 1.3150 stop loss and a 1.3060 take profit (60 pips), 20 percent of normal trade size.

The basic principles of staggered orders as I use them are: (1) the same entry level and stop loss are used for all orders, (2) Trade 1 is the largest in size and aims for the basic 40 pips target, (3) Trades 2 and 3 are smaller in size than Trade 1, and (4) Trades 2 and 3 each aim for an extra 10 pips over the previous trade. The maximum gain I aim for in Trade 3 is 60 pips, which is half of the average daily trading range of EURUSD. If all three staggered orders are profitable, I achieve 70 pips instead of 40. Conversely, if all three are negative trades, I could lose 0.8 percent of my account—which is within my 1 to 2 percent risk tolerance.

Final Thoughts

Now that you have come to the end of reading this book, I trust you are feeling eager to put these principles to the test. You should be pleased with yourself for having gained a solid foundation in currency trading, a lifelong skill that can bring you so many rewards. This skill can truly change your life for the better in a world that is full of uncertainty! I conclude with a recap of important points and some final thoughts.

CHAPTER TAKEAWAYS

This section is meant to help you recall the most important points of the book. You may want to highlight these concepts, which I hope will become clearer as you read the book a second time and/or talk to a trading coach.

Chapter 1. In the first chapter, I made the point that the processes of learning to drive and learning to trade proficiently bear striking similarities and are performed best when individuals follow basic rules. For both activities, it takes months to attain a level of proficiency, and both activities require patience. Citing Aite Group research, I showed that the number of forex traders worldwide is growing and that these traders are being drawn to this market by two main factors: (1) higher-than-average potential returns and (2) the appeal of a market that is highly liquid and resilient in the face of economic turmoil.

Chapter 2. In this chapter, I went over the basic terminology of forex trading, including the meaning of currency pairs, pips, and basic buy and sell operations (sell at the bid, buy at the ask). I also included explanations to help you grasp the relationship between currency spread and forex liquidity.

Chapter 3. In this chapter, you learned that a proper trader education requires carefully selected knowledge, tools, and support—not just the raw trading knowledge that can be found in such abundance through web searches. I reinforced the notion that the use of a practice account is of critical importance in the development of proficient traders and should not be something that you breeze through. We went over how demo trading teaches you patience and how to make the mental and emotional transition into trading with real money. This chapter also covered how to set performance targets, such as aiming for a net 20 pips per day (grossing 40 pips per day) while risking no more than 30 pips or 1 to 2 percent of the trading account. We also saw tables showing the type of potential returns that are within the reach of disciplined traders who keep their risk constant and reinvest their earnings for a period.

Chapter 4. In Chapter 4, you became familiar with the MT4 trading platform, the use of mini and standard lots, and the prudent use of margin. You were introduced to a sample leveraged trade, and you learned to measure risk and reward using the margin required and margin level. You also learned the wisdom of using only a small portion of your available credit to stay away from the dreaded margin call.

Chapter 5. This chapter gave you an early dose of technical analysis, covering basic concepts like chart types, candlesticks, and support and resistance lines. You learned how to recognize important chart patterns and some trading opportunities within them. We concluded this chapter by discussing the use of Fibonacci studies and how to apply them in the MT4 platform.

Chapter 6. This chapter was all about fundamental analysis. It started off with a warning about how forex liquidity dries up temporarily during major news events and why it is best to stay away from the market during these periods. One of the tables also helped you identify the major economic announcements you should track. We discussed how in freely floating currency markets, global markets set an adequate price in response to changes in the economy and in policies. You also learned about three major themes in currency markets: the U.S. dollar, the credit crises, and changes in interest and growth rates. We then named some of the people who, by virtue of their role, affect currency markets. The chapter concluded with a list of reliable indicators for gauging the sentiment among investors and in capital markets.

Chapter 7. In this chapter, we covered the book's primary trading strategy, the VT Pivot Roadmap strategy, in great detail. We started off with a basic overview of pivot lines and how certain tools, such as the VT Pivot Lines indicator, can make the job of drawing pivot lines much easier. We then went on to see how recurrent patterns, such as the pivot challenge, present trading opportunities. These opportunities became clearer as we examined the statistics and probabilities surrounding this strategy. The strategy then outlined three clear rules for determining whether to place a trade, and we touched on other basic points, including how to set appropriate trade sizes, profit targets, stop-loss levels, and limit orders. The chapter concluded by simulating the trading strategy in action during eight consecutive days.

Chapter 8. This chapter was the central part of the book. In it, you saw that a forex trading plan needs a high level of precision in a number of areas if it is to be of benefit to traders. These areas will be ultimately customized by you, based on what you feel comfortable with and what you feel you can commit to. Some of the areas included are trading goals, trading discipline, currency traded, trading schedule, trade size and risk management, and trading strategy. Another important area covered was a pretrade routine, which included (1) some regular activities (reading and making journal entries, gauging investor mood, looking at price barriers, and evaluating important economic events that have taken place or are upcoming), (2) some strategy-specific activities, and (3) basic risk-management principles. In addition, the trading plan included rules and clarifications concerning trade frequency, trade duration, charts, trade journal entries, mental conditioning, and account safeguards.

Chapter 9. Chapter 9 focused on the mental conditioning training that can help you make a successful transition to the thought patterns of proficient traders. It reveals how the mind has the power to accept or reject positive change. This section made reference to recent work by John Assaraf on how the mind works and how positive change can be achieved. Including a chapter on mental conditioning along with a successful strategy and a detailed trading plan is part of what will help readers make a transition to successful forex trading.

Chapter 10. Hopefully, Chapter 10 will prove to be a useful reference guide for the various types of needs you will have as a trader. The services and product categories listed include e-mail signals, forex news, economic calendars, trader education methods, trader education books, online trading rooms, advanced trading platforms, trader tools, trader magazines, and regulatory bodies.

Chapter 11. Closing out this book, Chapter 11 offered you two additional techniques for maximizing profitable trades: the use of trailing stops and staggered limit orders. There are conditions for using a trailing stop, such as attaching it at the right time, picking the right trailing stop size, and keeping the computer on while the trailing stop is active.

FINAL THOUGHTS

I've heard someone say that it does not matter what trading strategy you pick as long as you have sound risk management and try to be consistent in using whatever strategies you have chosen. I tend to agree with this view. Books have elements that are perennial and other parts that change over time and become somewhat dated. Although I realize that most trading strategies come and go, I feel very confident about the principles contained in the VT Pivot Roadmap strategy. I am even more confident about the three areas covered in this book: having a sound risk-management plan (risk-based trade size), a precise trading plan, and a clear understanding of the mental conditioning necessary to become a trader. The VT Pivot Roadmap applies specifically to EURUSD (and probably to the USD-German mark if we ever see it again). The other three principles that I described are perennial and apply to any currency pair or market that you may trade online: stocks, options, futures, and so on.

If you are just starting to trade, these are the next steps:

1. If you haven't already done so, download the MT4 trading platform. ForexDatasource.com offers a complementary download link at www.forexds.com /download/mt4platform. Once you have installed the platform, create two demo accounts: demo 1 (which follows the trading plan strictly) and demo 2 (used for experimentation and random trading impulses).

2. Complete a free registration at VaraTrade.com to gain three important benefits:
   a. Customize your forex news and keep track of important market developments.
   b. Get a digital copy of the trading plan format seen in Chapter 8—request it by e-mailing info@varatrade.com.
   c. Get a six-month license of the VT Pivot Lines indicator—request it by e-mailing info@varatrade .com.

3. Customize your own trading plan. Also customize your 30-day trader reconditioning plan following the six steps in Chapter 9, including creating a powerful personal declaration, affirmations, and visual and audible stimuli. Print these, and keep them handy for daily access.

4. Start trading and keeping a daily log of your trading activities. Consider using an electronic method to track your trading performance, such as registering for Myfxbook.com and/or getting the free version of TradeOnTrack.com.

5. Evaluate your performance every week or two and try to isolate potential problems. Adjust the trading plan, if necessary. Read this book once again after a month of trading to see what new insights you are able to gain.

I am confident in your ability to become a disciplined, proficient trader. I commend you for your determination to learn from the mistakes of others and to put the principles in this book into practice. I wish you the best. Trade safely!

How to Open a Practice Account

For our discussion of downloading the MT4 platform, I have selected the version offered by OANDA.

Here are the steps to install an MT4 trading platform.

To download an MT4 platform, go to www.forexds.com /download/mt4platform

- Click on the download link. This will start the installation process, and you will see a new small window appear that will guide you through the setup process.
- Prompt: "Do you want to save or run this file?" Click RUN.
- Prompt: "Choose installation language." Select English (United States) or your preferred language, and click NEXT.
- Click NEXT in the five screens that you see.
- The program will install in your machine.
- Click FINISH when the installation is complete.
- Find the MT 4 icon on your desktop and open it.

- You will see the MT4 platform open up. The first time you open the platform, you will see a small "Open an Account" window appear.
- If you do not see this window appear, you can click on the platform's File menu and then select "Open an Account."
- In this small window, enter some basic information, such as
  □ Your name, address, and other information.
- Select the account size "Deposit." I recommend that you enter a realistic amount of money that you would trade in real life after you finish your training—I usually select $10,000 or $50,000.
- Select the account leverage, usually 50:1.
- Check the little box "I agree to subscribe to your newsletters"; otherwise the account will not activate.
- Click NEXT two times, and then click FINISH.

Your practice trading account is now set up.

Let's say that you have used up a practice account, as the balance is now too low for your preference. In this event, you can easily open a new account: from inside the platform, click on FILE, then on "Open an Account"; then follow the prompts just as you did the first time.

Trade Size Table

Brought to you by VaraTrade.com

| ACCOUNT BALANCE | TRADE SIZE | | AMOUNT RISKED | MARGIN LEVEL |
| | MINI | STANDARD | 30 PIPS
1% | 50:1
EURUSD 1.30 |
	MINI LOTS	STD LOTS		
$500	0.2		$5	962%
$1,000	0.3		$10	1282%
$1,500	0.5		$15	1154%
$2,000	0.7		$20	1099%
$2,500	0.8		$25	1202%
$3,000	1.0	0.10	$30	1154%
$3,500	1.2	0.12	$35	1122%
$4,000	1.3	0.13	$40	1183%
$4,500	1.5	0.15	$45	1154%
$5,000	1.7	0.17	$50	1131%
$5,500	1.8	0.18	$55	1175%
$6,000	2.0	0.20	$60	1154%
$6,500	2.2	0.22	$65	1136%
$7,000	2.3	0.23	$70	1171%
$7,500	2.5	0.25	$75	1154%
$8,000	2.7	0.27	$80	1140%
$8,500	2.8	0.28	$85	1168%
$9,000	3.0	0.30	$90	1154%
$9,500	3.2	0.32	$95	1142%
$10,000	3.3	0.33	$100	1166%
$10,500	3.5	0.35	$105	1154%
$11,000	3.8	0.38	$110	1113%
$11,500	3.9	0.39	$115	1134%
$12,000	4.0	0.40	$120	1154%
$12,500	4.2	0.42	$125	1145%
$13,000	4.3	0.43	$130	1163%
$13,500	4.5	0.45	$135	1154%
$14,000	4.7	0.47	$140	1146%
$14,500	4.8	0.48	$145	1162%
$15,000	5.0	0.50	$150	1154%

| ACCOUNT BALANCE | TRADE SIZE | | AMOUNT RISKED | MARGIN LEVEL |
| | MINI | STANDARD | 30 PIPS | 50:1 |
	MINI LOTS	STD LOTS	1%	EURUSD 1.30
$15,500	5.2	0.52	$155	1146%
$16,000	5.3	0.53	$160	1161%
$16,500	5.5	0.55	$165	1154%
$17,000	5.7	0.57	$170	1147%
$17,500	5.8	0.58	$175	1160%
$18,000	6.0	0.60	$180	1154%
$18,500	6.2	0.62	$185	1148%
$19,000	6.3	0.63	$190	1160%
$19,500	6.5	0.65	$195	1154%
$20,000	6.7	0.67	$200	1148%
$20,500	6.8	0.68	$205	1160%
$21,000	7.0	0.70	$210	1154%
$21,500	7.2	0.72	$215	1149%
$22,000	7.3	0.73	$220	1159%
$22,500	7.5	0.75	$225	1154%
$23,000	7.7	0.77	$230	1149%
$23,500	7.8	0.78	$235	1159%
$24,000	8.0	0.80	$240	1154%
$24,500	8.2	0.82	$245	1149%
$25,000	8.3	0.83	$250	1158%
$25,500	8.5	0.85	$255	1154%
$26,000	8.7	0.87	$260	1149%
$26,500	8.8	0.88	$265	1158%
$27,000	9.0	0.90	$270	1154%
$27,500	9.2	0.92	$275	1150%
$28,000	9.3	0.93	$280	1158%
$28,500	9.5	0.95	$285	1154%
$29,000	9.7	0.97	$290	1150%
$29,500	9.8	0.98	$295	1158%
$30,000	10.0	1.00	$300	1154%

| ACCOUNT BALANCE | TRADE SIZE | | AMOUNT RISKED | MARGIN LEVEL |
| | MINI | STANDARD | 30 PIPS | 50:1 |
	MINI LOTS	STD LOTS	1%	EURUSD 1.30
$30,500	10.2	1.02	$305	1150%
$31,000	10.3	1.03	$310	1158%
$31,500	10.5	1.05	$315	1154%
$32,000	10.7	1.07	$320	1150%
$32,500	10.8	1.08	$325	1157%
$33,000	11.0	1.10	$330	1154%
$33,500	11.2	1.12	$335	1150%
$34,000	11.3	1.13	$340	1157%
$34,500	11.5	1.15	$345	1154%
$35,000	11.7	1.17	$350	1151%
$35,500	11.8	1.18	$355	1157%
$36,000	12.0	1.20	$360	1154%
$36,500	12.2	1.22	$365	1151%
$37,000	12.3	1.23	$370	1157%
$37,500	12.5	1.25	$375	1154%
$38,000	12.7	1.27	$380	1151%
$38,500	12.8	1.28	$385	1157%
$39,000	13.0	1.30	$390	1154%
$39,500	13.2	1.32	$395	1151%
$40,000	13.3	1.33	$400	1157%
$40,500	13.5	1.35	$405	1154%
$41,000	13.7	1.37	$410	1151%
$41,500	13.8	1.38	$415	1157%
$42,000	14.0	1.40	$420	1154%
$42,500	14.2	1.42	$425	1151%
$43,000	14.3	1.43	$430	1157%
$43,500	14.5	1.45	$435	1154%
$44,000	14.7	1.47	$440	1151%
$44,500	14.8	1.48	$445	1156%
$45,000	15.0	1.50	$450	1154%

| ACCOUNT BALANCE | TRADE SIZE | | AMOUNT RISKED | MARGIN LEVEL |
| | MINI | STANDARD | 30 PIPS 1% | 50:1 |
	MINI LOTS	STD LOTS		EURUSD 1.30
$45,500	15.2	1.52	$455	1151%
$46,000	15.3	1.53	$460	1156%
$46,500	15.5	1.55	$465	1154%
$47,000	15.7	1.57	$470	1151%
$47,500	15.8	1.58	$475	1156%
$48,000	16.0	1.60	$480	1154%
$48,500	16.2	1.62	$485	1151%
$49,000	16.3	1.63	$490	1156%
$49,500	16.5	1.65	$495	1154%
$50,000	16.7	1.67	$500	1152%
$50,500	16.8	1.68	$505	1156%
$51,000	17.0	1.70	$510	1154%
$51,500	17.2	1.72	$515	1152%
$52,000	17.3	1.73	$520	1156%
$52,500	17.5	1.75	$525	1154%
$53,000	17.7	1.77	$530	1152%
$53,500	17.8	1.78	$535	1156%
$54,000	18.0	1.80	$540	1154%
$54,500	18.2	1.82	$545	1152%
$55,000	18.3	1.83	$550	1156%
$55,500	18.5	1.85	$555	1154%
$56,000	18.7	1.87	$560	1152%
$56,500	18.8	1.88	$565	1156%
$57,000	19.0	1.90	$570	1154%
$57,500	19.2	1.92	$575	1152%
$58,000	19.3	1.93	$580	1156%
$58,500	19.5	1.95	$585	1154%
$59,000	19.7	1.97	$590	1152%
$59,500	19.8	1.98	$595	1156%
$60,000	20.0	2.00	$600	1154%

| ACCOUNT BALANCE | TRADE SIZE | | AMOUNT RISKED | MARGIN LEVEL |
| | MINI | STANDARD | 30 PIPS | 50:1 |
	MINI LOTS	STD LOTS	1%	EURUSD 1.30
$60,500	20.2	2.02	$605	1152%
$61,000	20.3	2.03	$610	1156%
$61,500	20.5	2.05	$615	1154%
$62,000	20.7	2.07	$620	1152%
$62,500	20.8	2.08	$625	1156%
$63,000	21.0	2.10	$630	1154%
$63,500	21.2	2.12	$635	1152%
$64,000	21.3	2.13	$640	1156%
$64,500	21.5	2.15	$645	1154%
$65,000	21.7	2.17	$650	1152%
$65,500	12.8	1.28	$655	1968%
$66,000	22.0	2.20	$660	1154%
$66,500	22.2	2.22	$665	1152%
$67,000	22.3	2.23	$670	1156%
$67,500	22.5	2.25	$675	1154%
$68,000	22.7	2.27	$680	1152%
$68,500	22.8	2.28	$685	1156%
$69,000	23.0	2.30	$690	1154%
$69,500	23.2	2.32	$695	1152%
$70,000	23.3	2.33	$700	1155%
$70,500	23.5	2.35	$705	1154%
$71,000	23.7	2.37	$710	1152%
$71,500	23.8	2.38	$715	1155%
$72,000	24.0	2.40	$720	1154%
$72,500	24.2	2.42	$725	1152%
$73,000	24.3	2.43	$730	1155%
$73,500	24.5	2.45	$735	1154%
$74,000	24.7	2.47	$740	1152%
$74,500	24.8	2.48	$745	1155%
$75,000	25.0	2.50	$750	1154%

Chapter 1

1. *Financial Times*, October 12, 2009.

Chapter 2

1. The Mesopotamian shekel was both a unit of currency and a standard weight for barley in 3,000 BC. In the first millennium before Christ, the use of cowrie shells and metal coins began to be widely adopted in ancient China, Africa, and Greece instead of commodities such as copper, wine, and rice, which were cumbersome to transport. These various instruments of exchange fostered domestic and international commerce.

Chapter 3

1. Other terms used for practice accounts are *demo account, simulated (sim) account, paper-trading account*, and *play money account*.

Chapter 4

1. There are brokers that show four decimal places in the MarketWatch window, with pips being the last value in the

sequence. For example, EURUSD at 1.2304 means that the fourth digit to the right of the period is the pip. The majority of brokers today show five decimal places for currency pairs, with the fifth digit being a fraction of a pip. So if the price for EURUSD is 1.23043, then this should be understood as 4.3 pips. If your broker displays five digits on prices and you want to stop the trade when you show a 20-pip profit, then in the profit/loss column, the price must show "200." Don't be surprised if during the coming year or two brokers begin showing 6 decimals on normal pairs and 4 decimals on pairs including the Japanese yen; this trend of more decimals already is taking place in Japan.

2. The calculation for the margin required (in U.S. dollars) is: 100,000 currency units × 0.97828 AUDUSD rate × 2% margin rate × 1 standard lot = $1,956.56. Whereas the rate is 2 percent in the United States, it varies by broker and country. A 1 percent margin rate applies in the United Kingdom and many other countries, while it goes up to 4 percent in places like Japan.

3. In the United States, as of October 2010, the CFTC (Commodity Futures Trading Commission; the principal forex regulator) set the maximum leverage at 50:1 for major currencies and 20:1 for less popular currencies. Brokers outside the United States offer a maximum leverage greater than 50:1, but the CFTC prevents foreign brokers from opening forex accounts on behalf of U.S. residents.

Chapter 5

1. Candlesticks can measure price movements in other intervals, with each candle representing the change in price over 1 minute, 5 minutes, 15 minutes, 30 minutes, 1 hour, 4 hours, 1 day, 1 week, or 1 month.

Chapter 6

1. It is actually more complicated than that. Factors affecting this kind of trade execution include partial fills at different prices, different bank quote durations, bad bank fills, and client and broker price latency.

Chapter 9

1. John Assaraf and Murray Smith, *The Answer* (New York: Simon & Schuster, 2008), p. 111.
2. Ibid., p. 115.
3. Ibid., p. 50.

Chapter 10

1. Certain proprietary trading programs invite individuals to pay fees of $10,000 to $30,000 to learn to trade well enough to eventually manage the proprietary funds of the company offering the trading instruction (the "trade our money" marketing approach). Again, I don't recommend this kind of program to anyone.

A

B

Javier H. Paz is a veteran forex trader and a recognized online trading industry expert. As senior analyst for Boston-based Aite Group, Javier evaluates trends in the active trading industry and is regularly quoted in the financial media (*Wall Street Journal*, Reuters, and Bloomberg). He has also served in trading-industry events as keynote speaker, judge, and panelist. Prior to Aite Group, Javier launched ForexDatasource.com, an independent research web portal helping sophisticated traders to find the most suitable retail FX brokers. Prior to this experience, he also ran the institutional desk of retail FX broker IBFX and worked as analyst in the fixed income and derivatives desk of Credit Suisse First Boston and BankBoston. Javier has traveled extensively, holds an MBA from Brigham Young University, and is fluent in English, Spanish, French, and Portuguese.